# Tell me the Story

## The Carpenter

*Alex J MacDonald*

CHRISTIAN
**FOCUS**

Copyright © Alex J MacDonald 2007

ISBN 978-1-84550-285-0

Published in 2007
by
Christian Focus Publications, Geanies House,
Fearn, Ross-shire, IV20 1TW, Scotland

www.christianfocus.com

Cover design by info@moose77.com

Printed and bound by CPD, Wales

Having heard the chapter on Joanna given as a Sunday evening sermon I can appreciate the living situation from which the skilful telling of these stories has come. They are a practical and helpful reminder that we often fail to capture people's imagination in telling the exciting story the narrative of the New Testament provides. The writer's motivation is that of an earnest communicator of the gospel who commendably tries every helpful approach to help his readers and listeners to understand the greatest good news there is.

*Derek Prime*
Former pastor of Charlotte Chapel, Edinburgh

I read these stories at a sitting and really enjoyed them. I understand now why people say that when Alex preaches these story-sermons you can hear a pin drop. And I also appreciate why by God's grace these same occasions are often when the penny drops. Good stories have a way of getting round people's carefully constructed defences. Through imaginative retelling, these tales bridge the centuries. We feel like contemporary witnesses, participants even, seeing the truth and feeling its power. May these stories draw many to the hero of the biggest story of all.

*Alasdair I Macleod*
St Andrews Free Church

Narrative preaching is an extremely difficult art to master, because imagination has to be used as a tool to convey truth and make the reader want to grasp it, but must never take over itself. Alex MacDonald has managed here to present us with a series of stories that superbly manage to retell well known historical facts in a way that magically take us to the lands and times in which they actually happened. A book for young and old, for seasoned preachers and truth-seekers, and ultimately for anyone who simply likes stories well told.

*Manuel Reaño*
Principal, Bible Seminary of Colombia
Medellin-Colombia, South America.

Should the Gospel be made available only in erudite style? Or, can the simple power of narrative also serve the Evangel in the lives of young and old? In his new book *Tell me the Story*, Alex MacDonald retells the ancient tale of Jesus in the contemporary tongue of narrative account. With delightful turn of phrase and surprising perspective, we are invited to hear afresh the storyline of the Gospel message. A faithful preacher with an eye towards making the Good News intelligible to everyman, Alex MacDonald warms our hearts with his fusion of timeless truth through vibrant imagination. These dozen eyewitness accounts of Bible figures and their companions will stir your heart to treasure again the old, old story of Jesus and His love!

*W. Duncan Rankin*
Senior Minister
Covenant Presbyterian Church
Oak Ridge, Tennessee

# Contents

# 1
# The Mother's Story

I was very young then – still in my teens. And now I'm old, and so much has happened. People often ask me about those days. But not so much now – not since Dr Lucas wrote down my story – you can read it all there, if you want.

But I don't mind telling you my story – in fact it's good to remember.

As I said, I was just a young girl when it all started to happen. They were dark times then. The King was a cruel tyrant. 'The Great,' they called him. Great in pride and in cruelty, if you asked me. O yes, he was famous for all the fine buildings he put up ... in Greek and Roman style. He even completely rebuilt our Temple, turning it into a great big one. Perhaps he thought people would think he was as great as Solomon! But it takes more than putting up fine buildings to make a man great. In any case, he thought nothing of building pagan temples as well. And do you know, before he died he had his wife and her sons put to death! At least she died before her sons ... poor woman.

It had been dark for a long time. There had been a ray of hope for a time when Judas Maccabaeus won our independence again. But it was only for a time, before the Romans came – and then they appointed Herod as King. He was a friend of the first Emperor – Augustus they called him. It's funny how they gave themselves such high sounding names – 'the Great' and 'Augustus' (His Reverence). Not like the name my son gave himself – the Son of Man – that was all.

Anyway, as I was saying, it was a dark time. There had been no word from the Lord for a long time – many lifetimes of men. Of course we had the Law, and the Prophets and the Writings, but they were all pointing forward to something – something much greater. There were great promises, you know – promises to Abraham – to make one of his descendants a great blessing to all the nations of the world – promises about the Lion of the Tribe of Judah, about a great Son of David who would set us free, rescue the poor and needy and put down the rich and proud.

There were some of us longing for that time. Many thought it was freedom from the Romans and from Herod. I thought that too then. But now ... a lot has changed since then. It's a different world.

You know, I'm descended from King David. So was my husband Joseph – descended directly from the line of the true kings of Israel. A people long forgotten, living in the shadows – while upstart high priests and kings lorded it over God's people. But it was not to them that Gabriel came – not to a daughter of Herod in his fine Palace nor to a daughter of the High Priest in Herod's Temple in Jerusalem, but to me! Yes, to me, a poor Nazareth girl engaged to be married to Joseph the carpenter!

A lot of people have asked me about Gabriel. 'What was it like to meet an angel?' they say. Well, it wasn't like what people imagine. It wasn't even like the experience the Bethlehem shepherds told me about later: bright, shining light – awesome, terrifying. He was quiet-like; spoke gently.

It wasn't what he looked like, but what he said that bothered me. He said I was highly favoured and the Lord was with me. You wouldn't even say that to some fine lady, and I was a nobody. He could see I was troubled and he said, 'Mary, don't be afraid.' He said I had found what I had been looking for all my life – the favour and the grace of God.

That's when he told me. He said I was going to have a baby. And not just any baby! He said I would have a son, and he told me what to name him – Joshua, or Jesus in the language of the West. He said God would give him the throne of his ancestor David and his kingdom would last forever.

But that's not all. He said he would be called the Son of God. I didn't know what he meant – then. I was struggling to take it all in. The return of the King! The birth of the Promised One. God was starting to move.

The waiting was over. The darkness was ending. And I was going to be his mother!

How did I feel?! I was shocked, astonished, dazed, delighted, scared. What did I say? Remember, I was only a teenager. And I've always been a very practical person. I said, 'How's this going to happen? I'm still a virgin!' You might think that's no way to talk to an angel, but I wanted to know! You see he never said a word about Joseph.

He said, 'The Holy Spirit will come upon you, and the power of the Most High will overshadow you. So the Holy One to be born will be called the Son of God.'

Then he told me about my old relative Elizabeth. She'd never been able to have children. And now, he said, she was six months pregnant. 'Nothing is impossible with God.' That's what he said.

That's when it finally dawned on me. I was going to have a baby. And no man was going to be involved. Not Joseph, not anyone. And my baby was going to be the One – the long promised Son of David!

I was scared, but I managed to say, 'I'm the Lord's servant. Let it happen just as you've said.' He seemed happy with that and he left.

Well, my mind was in turmoil. What was I going to do? I didn't know. I needed to talk to someone, but I couldn't talk to Joseph or my parents – I was scared of what they would think. It was just after that that the news came through from the hill country of Judea – about Elizabeth expecting! I realised this was the perfect opportunity. I said I wanted to go to help Elizabeth. Well, to cut a long story short, my parents and Joseph eventually all agreed it was a good idea. God was so good to me. He allowed me to go to see the one person in the world who would understand.

It was a long journey over the hills to her town near Jerusalem. I had a lot of time to think over what was happening. Words kept on coming into my mind. Then, when I arrived at Elizabeth's place, something strange happened. As soon as I shouted 'Hello,' she came out and said I was blessed among women. She called me the mother of her Lord and said her baby had jumped for joy inside her when he heard my voice! She knew. Don't ask me how, but she knew.

That's when it all burst out of me – all I'd been thinking over on the way there. I could hardly believe it was me talking. I'd never made a speech before. But all I kept thinking about was how God had blessed me – a nobody. God was turning the world upside down. The high and mighty were going to be brought down and the poor and the humble were going to be lifted up. It just all poured out of me. Elizabeth made me memorise it and she memorised it. She even got her husband to write it all down. He had been struck dumb, ever since Gabriel had announced his son's birth, but anyway he could hear and he could write. He had written down all that the angel had said to him and that their son was to be called John. You can read all about it in Dr Lucas' history – he copied it all down. A very clever man, Dr Lucas. A very nice man too… for a Greek!

But those three months with Elizabeth were great times – I stayed with her until her baby was born. And that was funny! Because his father couldn't speak, all the greybeards were going to name the baby Zechariah, after his father. Elizabeth said 'No! He's to be called John!' There was much shaking of heads at this, because that wasn't a family name. They asked Zechariah and to everyone's astonishment he wrote 'His name is John'! That's when he started to speak again, and it all burst out of him – just like it had with me. He said John would be a prophet and he would prepare the way of the Lord. He said the rising sun was coming from heaven to shine on those living in darkness and in the shadow of death.

When I went back to Nazareth, I knew what I had to do. I'd talked it over with Elizabeth. I had to tell Joseph. She said he would understand… eventually.

That was the worst time. He didn't understand at all. He was talking about breaking off the engagement. He said he would do it quietly. He didn't want me to be disgraced. (That was so like Joseph – always wanted to do the right thing, but didn't want to hurt anyone.) He just wouldn't listen. I suppose it was understandable. His girl was pregnant and he knew he wasn't the father. He couldn't seem to see past that. I cried myself to sleep that night. Everything seemed black again. Why was God allowing this to happen?

I don't know what would have happened, but that night God gave Joseph a dream. An angel told him there was nothing to be afraid of. He was to marry me. And he said exactly what Gabriel had said to me – my son was conceived by the Holy Spirit, and he was to be called Jesus (which means 'Saviour'), because he will save his people from their sins.

I don't mind saying there was a lot of crying and making up after that! And we did get married. And after Jesus was born we did have other children – James, Joseph, Judas and Simon, and the girls. But none of them were like him. How could they be?

But you wanted to know about his birth. He wasn't born in Nazareth where we lived. No, it was strange how it all come about in God's plan. This is where the Emperor comes in – Caesar Augustus sitting in Rome decides that there should be a census of the whole empire. And everyone had to go to his home town to register. Well, Joseph didn't come from Nazareth in Galilee. No, he came from Bethlehem in Judea, King David's town. So that's where we had to go. It was a long and difficult journey, with me nearly nine months pregnant. We had to be there before a certain date, and we just got there in time. In fact we couldn't find anywhere to stay, the place was so crowded. And nobody gave up their room for us. I thought that strange at the time – I looked very pregnant by then. But then, it's not just the high and mighty that stand on their rights, is it? A lot of people didn't have room for him then – and they still don't.

And that's why he was born in the stable and

his first bed was the animals' feeding trough. The innkeeper was a kindly man and he wouldn't turn us away completely. It wasn't the cleanest place to give birth, I suppose, but it was snug enough.

There was nothing special about the birth itself. I've given birth several times since then, and it was the same agony and the same elation on the birth of a healthy child. But it was special because he was special. I don't mean he didn't cry or need to be fed or changed like any other baby. He was just the same as far as all that goes. But he was the Firstborn. And not just *my* firstborn, if you understand. We knew who he was, only we didn't fully understand then.

We felt this awesome sense of responsibility as we wrapped him up and laid him in the manger. I know all parents do, but this was different. We were responsible for bringing up the one who would be known as the Son of David, the Son of the Most High. And here he was starting off in life in a stable!

But I suppose it was appropriate too. When he grew up he said he had come to preach good news to the poor. And God had already shown me that he was bringing down the proud and lifting up the humble. And you can't have more humble beginnings than he had.

And as if to emphasise that, that's when the shepherds came tumbling in. Now, I don't know about where you come from, but in our area shepherds were considered the lowest of the low. They had to be out in the hills in all weathers. They couldn't get to all the religious festivals. They were really considered outcasts. I always wondered about that, because our great ancestor Jacob was a shepherd, the prophet Moses was a shepherd and even King David was a shepherd. I was glad and proud later, when my Son said he was the good shepherd. It was as if he was restoring a lost dignity.

But there was nothing dignified about these shepherds. They were straight off the hills. And they were excited. They looked a cross between people who had seen a ghost and people who had seen the light!

They said, 'There he is. Just as the angel said. Wrapped up warmly, but lying in a manger. It's just like he said!' And they stood around looking sheepish (I don't know if shepherds can look sheepish, but these did!) We asked them what they meant. They needed some prompting, but eventually we got the whole story.

They had been guarding their sheep in the hills nearby, when all of a sudden the whole place was lit up, like lightning that just stayed there! And there was this angel. They were scared out of their wits, but he told them not to be afraid. He had been sent with good news of great joy for everyone. 'Today in the town of David,' he said, 'a Saviour has been born to you. He is the Messiah. He is the Lord. And you'll know it's true when you find him wrapped up, but lying in a manger!'

There was one word in all that that really stuck

in my mind. It was the word 'Saviour'. You see that's what I'd said that day at Elizabeth's house – 'God my Saviour.' And then that's what the angel had said to Joseph – he was to be called Jesus because he would save his people from their sins.

There was one last thing I should tell you. It happened six weeks later, the day we went up to the Temple in Jerusalem for my ceremony of purification after giving birth. There was an old man there called Simeon. He took my baby in his arms, and he prayed and told God he could let him die peacefully now, because he had seen his salvation! Then he turned to me – I'll never forget his words – he said, 'This child is destined to cause the falling and rising of many in Israel, and to be a sign that will be spoken against, so that the thoughts of many hearts will be revealed. And a sword will pierce your own soul too.'

Those were about the last words that old Simeon spoke to anyone, and they came true – every word! They came back to me that day – the day he was pierced. No mother should have to see that. And yet I wanted to be there. And I'm glad I was there. Even then he was concerned for me – got his friend John to look after me.

It was a crown of thorns he was wearing that day, but I thought he was more kingly than all the Herods and Caesars of this world. He has brought them down, but he has risen up and he has lifted up the poor and the humble with him.

Yes, I believe in him. I believe he is my Saviour. And

if I, his mother, who nursed him and cleaned him, believe that he is the Saviour of the world, the Son of God ... if his brothers and sisters, who fought and argued with him as he was growing up, can believe in him, I know you can too. All you have to do is accept you are poor and needy and guilty, and accept that he is the Saviour of sinners and ask him to forgive you.

# 2
# A Rock Cut from a Mountain

My name is Gaius Maximus. I was a centurion in the army of Quintilius Varus, governor of Syria at the time of the Jewish revolt after the death of King Herod.

After reigning for thirty-four years, Herod died from a loathsome disease in Jericho, some days after having one of his sons executed. In an eleventh hour revision to his will he left the kingdom to another son, Archelaus, who rightly wanted that confirmed by Caesar, so he set off for Rome.

That's when all Hades broke loose! Sabinus, the Treasurer, who had been sent by Caesar to make an inventory of Herod's estate, decided to plunder some for himself, and the people rose up in rebellion. So the army got sent in. It's always the same. It's the army who have to sort it out when the politicians mess it up! Even with two of the best legions at his command, Varus took some time to get everything under control again. But he ensured there wouldn't be much trouble for a while. He had two thousand of the rebels crucified.

But there were a lot of unanswered questions. It seemed there had been a lot of strange goings-on in the last days of Herod the Great (as they called him). Caesar wanted a report, so he could decide what to do about Archelaus, as there were competing claims for the throne. Another son, Antipas, was contesting Herod's will. So that's why Varus gave me a special commission to carry out an investigation and report directly to him. I suppose he chose me because of my local connections. Although my father was an army man, from Gaul originally, my mother was local. They met when he was stationed here during Pompey the Great's campaign.

There wasn't a lot of interesting stuff to report really. Just the usual stuff – palace intrigues, jealousies, scheming women, poisonings. Seemingly the old boy, Herod, had bumped off his favourite wife and her two sons – something about her being descended from a rival family. No wonder Caesar said, 'Better to be one of Herod's pigs than a son!'

Oh, and Herod's last illness was bizarre. Got all the gory details from his doctor. Swelled up to twice his normal size, seemingly.

However, there was *one* interesting thing. I kept hearing reports about one 'born King of the Jews' shortly before Herod's death. I thought it might be important, so I followed it up. Involved quite a bit of cloak and dagger stuff. My local connections helped me there. A certain innkeeper was a great source of information. He called his place *The House of Bread*. It was a bit of a joke, because that was the name of the town in the local lingo – *Bethlehem*. You know, House of Bread, an inn – get it? Oh well, never mind. He thought it was funny anyway.

The first he knew about all this was one night a young couple turned up on his doorstep. Well, the man was a bit older, but she was just a girl and very pregnant – about to give birth any minute. This placed him in a tricky position. All the rooms were taken. This was at the time of the Census that Caesar had ordered throughout the whole empire and everyone had to return to their home towns to be registered. The place was packed with people.

Anyway, he took pity on them. He was a decent sort of fellow really ... for an innkeeper! He gave them shelter in his stable. Warm enough, I suppose, with all the animals. And that's where it happened. That's where the baby was born – born safe and sound. The only cot they could find for him was a manger – you know, an animal's feeding box. I suppose it was just the right size. So they wrapped him up and put him in that.

Now, you might be wondering why an old soldier like me is telling you all this baby stuff. Well, it turns out that this was significant, but you'll just have to be patient and listen!

Now where was I? Yes, they were all settling down again, when there was this tremendous commotion. A bunch of herdsmen had rolled into town – you know, cowboys – only it was sheep they looked after, not cows, so I suppose they were shepherds, but you know the kind I mean. And they usually mean trouble.

The Innkeeper was not at all pleased about being kept even longer from his bed – especially not by that wild bunch. He would have locked the door in their faces, but there was something different about them. They looked as wild as ever, if not wilder, but they looked like they'd seen a ghost, and they asked if a baby had been born, as they had an important message about him, but only if it was the right child! He asked them how they would know if it was the right child. And they said he would be wrapped up but lying in a manger. He said a shiver ran up his spine when he heard that, and he asked them how they knew. They got even more excited at that and demanded to see the baby first, then they would tell all.

There was nothing for it but to agree or he would get no sleep that night, so he showed them into the stable. At first they were awkward and dumbstruck. Then they kept pointing at the baby and saying 'It's just like he said! It's just like he said!' Then they told their story.

I actually managed to trace one of them – I finally ran him to ground at a market outside Jerusalem – and he told me the same story as the innkeeper. It's a funny thing. I know when someone's telling the truth, especially when I've put the fear of death in them. And yet the story he told was incredible. I don't know what it was, but *something* happened that night in the hills outside Bethlehem, the Town of Bread. This is what he said.

They were guarding their flocks near Bethlehem one night, when they were scared out of their wits. The whole sky lit up around them and a messenger of the gods (well he said 'messenger of God' – they only believe in One) ... this messenger appeared to them, telling them not to be afraid, because he had good news for them and for the whole world. He said that very day in King David's Town a Saviour had been born for them – the Lord Christos. And he told them they would know the baby because he would be warmly wrapped up but lying in a manger!

I began to prick up my ears at all this, because 'Saviour' and 'Lord' were some of Caesar's titles. I once saw a public notice that said: 'It seemed good to the Greeks of Asia to give thanks for providence sending Augustus as a saviour and that his appearance surpassed expectations, since the birthday of the god was the beginning of the good news for the world.'

It seemed exceedingly strange to me that this peasant in another part of the world should use almost exactly the same language! What was going on? This word Christos, I found out, was also a title. It meant the anointed King of the Jews descended from the great King David. But it was clear someone was making very great claims for this baby. It wasn't just *Herod's* throne that was under threat. I started thinking this might be of more importance than anyone realised.

Talking of Herod reminds me of something. Something I noticed the first day I arrived in that place – the Town of Bread, Bethlehem. There were no little boys. I wondered about that, and my enquiries led me to the next part of the story. Seemingly Herod had them all killed! The local people were a bit cagey about it at first, but I got the truth out of them in the end, and I followed it up. There were no official records, but I spoke to some of the soldiers involved, and it was right enough. They didn't like talking about it – it was dirty work. No soldier likes doing that sort of thing – at least no real soldier. But 'orders is orders', as they say. But it does make you wonder what sort of rulers we have. Maybe we do need a new kind of kingdom.

Anyway, it all came about because of some visitors from the East. Some people thought they were kings – but I think that's because of the expensive gifts they brought. In reality they were stargazers, astrologers from the Land of the Two Rivers. They certainly must have been well off, because they travelled hundreds of miles at their own expense, or else their rulers sent them on a diplomatic mission.

Whatever. They arrived in the capital Jerusalem and, boy, did they cause a stir! They said they wanted to see the one born King of the Jews. They'd seen his star in the east and had come to worship him! (I got all this from a contact in Herod's palace and also from one of the religious leaders.)

King of the Jews. They might as well have announced the end of the world! The whole city was in an uproar and, when he heard about it, Herod hit the roof. (He was already ill by this stage and quite paranoid.) Seemingly 'King of the Jews' was a title for Christos – the King descended from David. Only there was a slight problem. Herod already was the King of the Jews!

Once he'd calmed down, he pretended to be really interested. He saw a way to use these stargazers to help him get rid of this rival. He summoned the religious experts and asked them where Christos was supposed to be born. They consulted their holy books and prophecies, and do you know what they came up with? Yes, you've guessed it – our old friend the House of Bread, Bethlehem! The holy man I interviewed showed me the exact spot in the scroll of the prophet Micah and this is what it said:

> But you, Bethlehem, in the land of Judah, are by no means least among the rulers of Judah; for out of you will come a ruler who will be the shepherd of my people Israel.

Strange that. Seemingly these words were written seven hundred years before, and now they seemed to be coming true. At any rate, all roads led to Bethlehem.

When Herod heard this, he swore the priests to secrecy and summoned the stargazers for a private audience. He was going to have to move carefully if he wasn't going to stir up a revolution.

He got the stargazers to do his detective work for

him, the crafty old fox. Sent them off to make a careful search and then come back and report to him when they had found the child. He wanted to worship him too, he said. Aye, right!

Oh yes, and he found out exactly when the star had appeared. That was his insurance policy if the stargazers didn't come back. He'd at least know what age of child to look for and in what town. I began to feel sorry for that child.

As it turned out the stargazers didn't make it back to Jerusalem. They vanished. No one in Jerusalem heard of them again. Herod was incandescent! He ordered out a detachment of soldiers with orders to slaughter all the male children under two years old in Bethlehem and the surrounding area. The soldier I interviewed said they carried out their orders to the letter. None escaped.

So that was it. Case closed. All those fine hopes came to nothing. No one was going to replace Herod, not while he was alive. It all seemed so pointless. He died a few weeks later. Not much of a kingdom he has now. A cold tomb. Let him rot in it, I say.

That would have been it really. I had a lot of other business to take care of before I could make my report to Varus. But in the course of all that, I had to visit Bethlehem again. So I thought I'd drop in and see my old friend the Innkeeper. We got talking and I asked him something that had been bothering me. He had never said anything about the stargazers. Had they never made it to Bethlehem? He said there had been no stargazers when the family were at his place, but they hadn't been there long. They managed to find a place to stay somewhere else in Bethlehem. My curiosity was roused and I got him to put me in touch with the people they'd stayed with, and after a bit of carrot and stick I got the story.

The stargazers *had* come and had traced the family. Something about the Star appearing again. Anyway, they bowed down and worshipped the child and then they gave him presents – expensive presents – gold and two very expensive kinds of perfume. Gold for a king, they said, frankincense for a priest and myrrh for one who was going to die.

That was thoughtful, I said, as Herod was going to have him killed. That's when the man and his wife exchanged glances. And that's when I decided to take a chance. I told them the file was closed. As far as my boss was concerned the child had been killed and that was the end of it. But I was curious to know myself. I kind of hoped the child had escaped.

They looked me straight in the eye and said they believed me. Then they told me what happened. The child *would* have been killed with all the others, were it not for a couple of dreams. First, one of the stargazers had a bad dream about King Herod, and they decided to hightail it back to their own country by a roundabout route.

And then the child's father had a dream. He got a message from God warning him to get out of there that very night. And that's what they did. They headed south by the desert road to Egypt, and they hadn't been seen or heard from since.

All the while they were talking the hairs on the back of my neck were standing on end. Part of me was glad. Glad he got away. And part of me was disappointed. I would never find them now – not in Egypt. The city of Alexandria alone has one million people.

But they did tell me something. They put me in touch with a relative of the mother – a woman called Elizabeth, who lived not far from Jerusalem in the hill country of Judea, with her husband, Zacharias. Now, *he* was an impressive old man. There was no fear in his eyes as he looked at *me*, Gaius Maximus, a centurion in the army of Augustus Caesar. It was as if his eyes had seen another glory.

I had a long talk with them. They didn't know where the family were, but they filled me in on a lot of the background. There were bigger things afoot than I had ever dreamed of.

Before I left, Zacharias caught me by the arm and this is what he said.

'You serve King Caesar. His kingdom is a kingdom of iron, but it has feet of clay. A Rock has been cut from a mountain, and one day soon that Rock will smash the feet of clay. Who will you serve then, Gaius Maximus? Will you serve the King of Kings?'

There was a time when I would have had him arrested and crucified for such rebellious talk, but not now. I was fed up with all the killing and slaughter, the cruelty, the lies, the filth. Maybe it was time for a change, for a new kind of king and a new kind of kingdom.

# 3
# A Voice in the Wilderness

It was about three years after I first heard him, that I actually understood what he was talking about. You might think that strange. But of course it sometimes takes a long time for something to sink in – especially something as big as what he was talking about. And then of course I saw it with my own eyes.

'A voice in the wilderness' – that's all he said he was, nothing more, taking up the words of the prophet written long ago. It was literally true, of course. If you wanted to see him you didn't go up to the capital city or even to one of the towns. You had to go out into the wilderness areas around the Jordan to see him. But such was his power that thousands did.

Of course he was a voice crying in the wilderness in another sense too. We were living in a wilderness – a spiritual wilderness. I know I was. In spite of the fact I was married to one of the most powerful men in the kingdom. I suppose I should have introduced myself – Joanna's my name, and my husband is

Khooza, King Herod's Chamberlain, his right hand man. O, don't get me wrong – we had all the wealth and influence anyone could ask for, but I wasn't happy – there was something missing. There was no peace. Instead there was fear. Fear of losing everything. Fear of palace intrigues. Fear of King Herod Antipas whose mood could change in a moment. But worst of all was his wife, Herodias. *There* was a woman who knew how to get her own way and would stop at nothing to get it. That's how everything went badly wrong in the end. I was so afraid and worried, I started drinking too much. That only made things worse. I made a fool of myself, and then I couldn't remember what I'd said to people.

But I suppose I should really start at the beginning.

It all started because of King Herod's suspicions. He liked to know everything that was going on in his kingdom, particularly anything that would cause trouble for him with the Romans. Because, although he wanted everyone to call him king, he was really only a puppet ruler, a Tetrarch (ruling a quarter of the Kingdom of Herod the Great, his father), and only by the leave of the Romans.

Anyway, when he heard of thousands of his subjects going down to the Jordan River to this preacher, he wanted to find out what was going on, so he sent my husband. And he asked me if I wanted to go along. I jumped at the chance to get away from the Palace for a while. At the time we were staying in the royal fortress of Machaerus and, although it was in a pleasant enough location high on the east side of the Dead Sea, and it was a long thirty miles journey down into the deep Jordan valley to the north, it was just good to get away from the place.

It was easy to find the preacher. Everyone was heading down to the Jordan – hundreds, thousands. But if it hadn't been for my husband's influence, we would never have got near enough to see him. As it was, we sat on a little grassy hill where we could see and hear everything.

What struck you first was his appearance. He looked wild! He wore a rough camel-hair coat with a leather belt and he ate whatever he could find in the wild – very different from the clothes and food I was used to at the royal court. Seemingly his elderly parents had died when he was quite young and he had lived in the desert ever since. His name was John.

I couldn't take my eyes off him. And it wasn't just because he looked weird. I had never heard anyone speak like him. He was like one of the old prophets come back to life – like Moses or Elijah. He said exactly what he thought and he didn't care what people said. How different from what we were used to in the Palace! Flattery. Gossip. Intrigue. Insinuation. By contrast, John spoke with overpowering authority, straight from the shoulder, and he didn't mince his words. Some of the religious leaders were there and he called them a 'bunch of snakes'. I laughed at that – to see those old hypocrites squirming. And they couldn't say a thing! No one would have heard them if they had – because what a voice he had! It was like thunder, it was like the sound of doom.

But no one escaped. Tax collectors, soldiers, everyone. He exposed wrongdoing and corruption everywhere. And he told us to start doing what was right – someone with two shirts should give one to someone who had none, and those with food should share with those who hadn't. I just knew he was right. The waste from the Palace kitchen for just one of our feasts would feed a whole village for months.

But he kept on telling us to get ready. It was a time of crisis. He could see the wrath of God coming like a flood that would sweep everything away. But he was sent to tell people the long awaited kingdom of God was near. To be part of it we had to turn from sin to God, and as a sign of our change of heart we had to be washed by him in the river! That sounded really strange, but you know I almost wanted to do it, right then. I know my husband wouldn't have allowed it, but it would have felt so good – to be washed clean from all the corruption and filth and shame.

But many people did go down to him in the River, and they weren't the people you'd expect – not the religious people, but prostitutes and drunkards and tax-collectors (whom the people regarded as no better than traitors). They confessed they'd sinned against God, and then he poured water over their heads and said their sins were forgiven. He said other things quietly to them, which we couldn't hear. And when they came up out of the river their faces were radiant – I'd never seen people with that kind of joy, and I envied them.

When the crowds were thinning out, some of the religious leaders plucked up courage to ask him who he thought he was that he could claim such things. Was he the Messiah – the long awaited descendant of King David – who would set up God's kingdom? At this my husband pricked up his ears. This was exactly the kind of thing Herod would be interested in. But John said, 'No! I am not! And neither am I Elijah nor one of the old prophets come back to life!'

'Who are you then?' they asked, 'And what authority have you got to say and do these things, if you are not the Messiah?'

John fixed them with his eye, and said, 'I am just the voice of one crying in the wilderness, "Prepare the way of the Lord."' He paused, and then he said – and a shiver went up my spine when he said it – 'I cleanse with water, but among you stands one you do not know, who will cleanse with the Holy Spirit and with fire.'

By this stage my husband wanted to go. He'd seen and heard enough. None of it had the same effect on him as it had on me. All he was interested in was that John was not claiming some political power. He had something to report to Herod. He didn't seem to understand the really revolutionary nature of what John was saying. I'm not saying I really understood it either, but I knew I'd heard something new and I wanted to hear more. There wasn't going to be much chance of that. As we made our way back up into the mountains, I went with a heavy heart.

Some months passed. I don't remember much about them – it was just a drunken haze. But I do remember that we'd been back in Tiberias, in one of Herod's other palaces by the Sea of Galilee. I liked it there. I was nearer my parents, although my mother wasn't all that well. But we were on our way back to Machaerus with the royal entourage, when Herod heard that John was nearby at a place called Aenon near Salim in the Jordan valley. Nothing would do but we had to make a detour – he had become obsessed with John, ever since my husband reported back to him.

John was in full flow as the royal party drew up. There weren't as many people around as before. Herod listened respectfully, although Herodias was muttering and sneering.

I was glad to see a friend of mine among those there and I managed to make an excuse and slip off to see her – Susanna from Galilee. I asked her all about what was happening. Seemingly she had been following John for some time. I asked her why there weren't so many people around. And she said something very interesting had happened. It was really John's own doing. One day his cousin, someone called Joshua, or Jesus in Greek, had come to be baptised by John, and John had said he wasn't worthy to baptise him – it should be the other way round. But Jesus told him to do it. And it was different from any other baptism. Some people said they saw something in the shape of a dove fall on Jesus from heaven, and some said they heard a voice from heaven – something about being God's own Son!

And then, Susanna said, one day John was with two of his followers and he pointed to Jesus and said, 'Look! The Lamb of God who takes away the sin of the world!' When she said that, something jumped inside me. I didn't understand it properly, but I knew all about the sin of the world and this was what I was looking for – something to take it away.

Anyway from that time on, people started leaving John and following Jesus, and John didn't mind. In fact he encouraged it. He said he was just the best man, Jesus was the bridegroom! He said, 'He must increase; I must decrease.'

Susanna herself had started to follow Jesus, and she said he was wonderful. He had helped her. I knew she had had a lot of trouble in her life, and she seemed different. She had a joy and peace I didn't know.

Just then John finished baptising, and I had to leave Susanna in case the Royal party were about to leave, but Herod sent a servant to John with a message that he was commanded to appear before the King. John duly came. In spite of all the snide remarks of the courtiers and Herodias wrinkling her nose and her daughter Salome sniggering at John's rough clothes, John looked more at ease than any of them.

Herod questioned him closely. He'd obviously

been paying close attention to what John had been saying. Herod was particularly interested in what John had been saying about the kingdom of heaven and how you had to repent to get into it. He asked if everyone needed to repent and when John said yes, he asked if that included King Herod as well. John never hesitated or blinked. He said that because King Herod was a sinner like everyone else, he too had to repent. You could hear a pin drop when Herod asked how he had sinned. John looked him straight in the eye and said, 'Your Majesty has sinned in many ways, not least in that you have been unfaithful to your first wife and stolen your brother's wife, Herodias, and married her.' At that there was a hysterical outburst from Herodias and her ladies. You could see Herod was angry and shaken, but I don't think he would have done anything worse than dismiss John with a warning. But Herodias made such a fuss that in the end John was dragged away by the guards and he was taken with us to the dungeons of Machaerus.

That didn't satisfy Herodias of course. She wanted John dead, but Herod drew the line at that, and in fact he infuriated his wife by occasionally bringing John out of the dungeons for an audience. And John never compromised, never toned down his message. Partly Herod was afraid of John, because he recognised he was a better man than himself – a godly and holy man. Partly he was fascinated with the things John had to teach – Herod had never really understood what the prophets had said. And partly he was disturbed by the challenging nature of John's preaching. He didn't know what to do with him.

Sometimes I would visit John and I discovered that he was beginning to have doubts, doubts about Jesus – about whether he was the one the prophets had spoken about. It wasn't because prison was getting to John – he was used to hardship. It wasn't because he was fickle and prone to change his ideas. It was because he was impatient. Impatient for the promises to be fulfilled. And nothing seemed to be happening. No kingdom was being set up. The Romans and Herod were still ruling.

In the end he sent two of his disciples (who were allowed to visit him) to see Jesus and to ask him, 'Are you the one who was to come, or should we expect someone else?'

It was some time before the messengers got back, but I was there the day they did. They reported they had asked Jesus John's question. And at first Jesus said nothing. He went on doing what he had been doing – healing people with diseases and illnesses, and giving the blind their sight back. Then he told the messengers, 'Go back and report to John what you have seen and heard: The blind receive sight, the lame walk, those who have leprosy are cured, the deaf hear, the dead are raised, and the good news is preached to the poor. Blessed is the man who does not fall away on account of me.'

They also heard that after they had left, Jesus had spoken to the crowd about John:'What did you go out into the desert to see? A reed swayed by the wind? If not, what did you go out to see? A man dressed in fine clothes? No, those who wear expensive clothes and indulge in luxury are in palaces. But what did you go out to see? A prophet? Yes, I tell you, and more than a prophet. This is the one about whom it is written: "I will send my messenger ahead of you, who will prepare your way before you." I tell you, among those born of women there is no-one greater than John; yet the one who is least in the kingdom of God is greater than he.'

At that John bowed his head and wept. After that day he had no more doubts.

It was not long after that that things reached a crisis. It was the night of King Herod's birthday. He had laid on a huge feast and all the important men of his kingdom were there. As the revelry wore on, Salome came in and shamelessly danced before them. They were all delighted with this, and Herod in a drunken stupor vowed she should have a great gift. He would give her anything up to half his kingdom! The girl was stunned, but she hurried out to her mother who knew exactly how to take advantage of the situation. In fact it wouldn't surprise me if she had set up the whole thing.

Salome came back in and smiling sweetly said, 'I want John the Baptist's head!' There were roars of laughter and ribald jokes from the guests. They started chanting, 'John's head! John's head!' Herod turned deathly pale. He was trapped and he couldn't see any way out. He hadn't the wit or the courage to say John's head was worth more than half his kingdom.

It's a terrible thing to see a poor weak-willed man with a loud conscience cracking under the pressure. He gave the order, but he was never the same man again.

The executioner brought back John's head on a plate and gave it to Salome, who gave it to her mother. It was a gruesome sight, but John's eyes still stared out defiantly, and there were none who could endure that stare, not even Herodias.

Some time later we went back to Tiberias – Herod could not endure Machaerus any longer. And I fell out of favour at court and returned home to nurse my mother who was dying. She told me of the wonderful things Jesus had been doing, and after she died I asked Susanna to introduce me to him. Although I'd left the corrupt influence of the Court, it had not left me and I was still drinking to excess. But from the day I met Jesus and he laid his hands on me and told me to be free, all craving for wine left me, and I knew my sins, which were many, were forgiven.

From then I followed Jesus, and it so happened we were up in Jerusalem at the end. I was with my husband in Herod's Palace there, but I was free to come and go as I pleased. So I was there with the other women from Galilee, Mary Magdalene and the others, that day the sky turned black. That day when we saw Jesus on the cross and heard him cry out, 'My God, my God, why have you forsaken me?' and I remembered John's words – 'Look, the Lamb of God who takes away the sin of the world!'

And yes I was there three days later when Mary, and I and some others went early on the first day of the week to pay our respects at the tomb of Jesus, and we found the stone rolled away and the grave empty.

John did no miracle, but all he said of this man was true!

# 4
# He Understands Me

It was a day much the same as any other really – cooking, washing, cleaning, looking after my man and my children. Then around the middle of the day I went as usual to fetch water from the well. There were several wells round our town. And although it was a good walk outside the town, I always went to Jacob's Well. I liked it there. I liked the fact that our ancestor Jacob himself, nearly two thousand years before, had dug that well and drank water from it.

It was quieter there too. Not so many people about – especially at the hottest part of the day. You see, people didn't really approve of me. So to avoid the hassle and the embarrassment, I just went there at that time of the day.

Why didn't they approve of me? Well, that's a long story. Let's just say I'd broken the rules. Respectable women didn't want to be seen on the same road as me, or let their daughters speak to me. It hurt. And it made me angry sometimes. Some of them wouldn't

43

have been so proud if I'd told them that there had been times when their husbands hadn't been so shy of speaking to me!

Anyway, going to the well was just part of the daily grind, and it made me feel how alone I really was. But this day was different. When I arrived at the well, I wasn't alone. There was a stranger sitting there. Judging by his dusty and tired appearance, he'd travelled quite a distance. As I got up closer I saw he was a Jew, so I expected him to get out of there fast when he saw me coming!

Perhaps I'd better explain. His people, the Jews, and my people, the Samaritans, had a history. We both trace our ancestry to Jacob, but they are descended mainly from Jacob's son, Judah, whereas we are descended mainly from another of Jacob's sons, Joseph. Away back, hundreds of years ago, all the twelve tribes descended from Jacob's twelve sons formed one kingdom under King David and then King Solomon, but after Solomon's death, there was trouble and the kingdom was divided between Judah in the south, around Jerusalem, and Israel in the north, with its capital city of Samaria. Later, when the mighty Assyrian Empire arose, they conquered Israel, exiled the upper classes and brought in other peoples. Then, when Babylon arose, the Jews in the south were also conquered and taken away, but seventy years later they were brought back, by the Persian emperor, King Cyrus. From that time on there was trouble between us. We wanted to help the Jews rebuild their temple in Jerusalem, but they didn't want our help. So we built our own temple on Mount Gerizim, just beside Sychar where I live. But then, after the time of Alexander the Great, when the Jews got independence again, they destroyed our temple. Even although we believed we had the right version of the Five Books of Moses, they wouldn't accept us. They said we were of mixed ancestry, we were descended from idolaters and they wouldn't have anything to do with us – they wouldn't even use the same cups and plates as us!

Imagine my surprise then, when this stranger, this Jew, asked me for a drink. I was nearly speechless (and that's something that doesn't happen very often – ask my man). It wasn't just that he was a Jew, but he was a Jewish man – and respectable Jewish men just didn't speak to women in public, and certainly not women like me!

I just managed to gasp, 'But you're a Jew! How can you ask for a drink from me – a Samaritan woman?' And I reminded him that Jews won't even use cups we have used. Actually I was quite pleased – I wasn't used to people speaking to me so pleasantly, and it was quite exciting to speak to this stranger at the well. I was thinking of some of the stories in the Five Books of Moses about people meeting at a well – about Jacob meeting his bride-to-be Rachel, and even of Hagar, Abraham's runaway servant girl (whom he had got pregnant) being met by God. She was an outcast too.

But it did puzzle me why he spoke to me at all and was prepared to share my water pot. Anyway, he never batted an eyelid. He didn't get angry. He just smiled and, as I started to lower my water pot down into the well, he went on speaking to me. He said something strange. He said, 'If you knew the gift of God and who was asking you for a drink, you would ask him and he would give you living water.' At least I know *now* that's what he meant, because the word he used for *living* water could have meant fresh, running water. So I said, 'But you don't have anything to draw water with, and this well is really deep. Where are you going to get this living water?' And then I was a bit cheeky. I was beginning to enjoy this conversation. I was more and more intrigued by this interesting stranger. As I drew the water up, I said, 'Are you greater than Jacob, who gave us this well and who drank from it with all his family and his flocks and herds?'

He laughed, and as I handed him the water he said something even more mysterious. I was standing over him waiting for him to have his drink. But he held the water pot in his hands and looked at the water sparkling in the sun as if it was the only thing in the world, and said, 'If you drink this water, you'll be thirsty again.' Then he looked up at me, and he looked at me as if I was the only person in the world, and he said, 'But if you drink the water I give you, you'll never thirst again. The water I give you will become a spring of water inside you welling up to everlasting life!'

As he said that, I felt a stab of joy and pain in my

heart. I know I didn't really understand what he was on about, but I knew the never-ending daily grind of fetching water, drinking water, fetching water. I knew only too well what it was not to be satisfied – and not just by water. I wanted to be loved, but felt I had never really been loved. And I knew he was meaning something religious. I knew religious people talked about everlasting life – life after death and all that. Sometimes I wished I was dead, but then I was afraid too. What really lay beyond the grave, if anything? No one *really* knew. But I knew the longing for a better life than this.

I looked at him hard as he took a long drink from the jar. I didn't quite know what to make of him. I didn't want to give too much away. So I smiled and said, 'Please give me that kind of water so I won't get thirsty and I won't have to keep coming back here to get water!' I suppose it was a stupid thing to say really, but I couldn't think of anything else. I was a bit flummoxed, which was not usual for me.

That's when he caught me off guard. He completely changed the subject. He told me to go and bring my husband to see him. That was going to be impossible. Because, truth be told, I hadn't been short of husbands, but none of them had stuck around, and the man I was with then was not my husband. But I wasn't about to tell *him* all that, so I just blurted out, 'I've no husband.'

He looked at me strangely, a bit like a father looking at a naughty child who had just told a lie, but he said, 'You're quite right. That's quite true. You don't have a husband.' He paused and added, 'But the whole story is you've been married five times and now you're living with another man!' He didn't say it in a sneering way. He didn't use the horrible names other people called me. He didn't say it in an accusing tone of voice. He just said it, matter of fact, like.

For a few moments I was speechless. I just stared at him. At one level it hurt – to be reminded of all that. It seemed so shameful. Of course I'd felt the shame before, but never as keenly as I did standing before this stranger. Somehow it mattered what *he* thought of me.

But there was an even bigger problem. How could he know all that? I'd never seen him before in my life. I was quite sure he'd never been to our town before. A Jewish Rabbi like him couldn't have visited without everyone knowing about it – such things just didn't happen. So how did he know all about me? My brain was working overtime. This was no ordinary Jew. Who was he? Was he, after all, greater than Jacob?

So I said, 'You must be a prophet!' No sooner were the words out of my mouth than I realised that here was someone who could answer my question. It wasn't that I just wanted to change the subject – although, to be honest, I did feel more comfortable talking about something else. But really this question had always bothered me. So I just came out with it. I said, 'Our ancestors worshipped here on Mount Gerizim, but you Jews say Jerusalem is the only place to worship

God.' That always bothered me. I would like to have believed in God and worshipped him properly, but I didn't know who to believe. One religion said this and another said that.

I was frightened he wouldn't actually talk to me anymore, knowing what he did about me, but of course that was stupid, because he already knew all that before he even asked me for a drink.

I needn't have worried. He answered my question, and he gave me a straight answer. He said, 'Very soon you're not going to worship the Father either on this mountain or in Jerusalem!' He called God 'the Father', and for some reason when he said that, my own father's face came into my mind. He died when I was just a girl. Maybe things would have turned out differently if he hadn't died ... but then who's to know?

Anyway, he didn't just call God Father, he said, 'Everything has changed. The time has come for a new kind of worship. You Samaritans worship him, but you don't know him. We do know the Father, and salvation is coming from the Jews, but God is Spirit and if you're going to worship him, you've got to worship him in spirit and in truth. That's the kind of worshippers the Father wants.'

I'd never heard anything like that before. I didn't understand it all then. I don't know if I understand it all yet! And there were some things hard to accept, like we didn't know God – but I knew he was right. *I didn't know God anyway.*

And everything he said reminded me of something both Jews and Samaritans believed in. We both were expecting Someone special who would come and put us right. We called him the Restorer, because God had said to Moses that he would raise up a prophet like him. And the Jews called him the Anointed King (or Christ), because God had said to King David that he would raise up a king from his family whose kingdom would never end. So I said, 'I know that the Christ is coming, and he'll tell us everything.'

He looked right into my eyes and said, 'I am the Christ!'

My heart gave a wild leap. I stood astonished before him, trying to take it all in – that the Great One should make himself known to me, the despised outcast! Could it really be true?

Just then his friends came back from the town with food. I realised they'd passed me on the way in as I was walking to the well. Although they didn't say anything, they seemed very surprised to see him talking to a woman alone – and a Samaritan woman at that! I took the chance to make myself scarce. I wanted to get back quickly to the town and tell everyone. I didn't want them missing out on the greatest thing that would ever happen in our country.

As I went back, half running, half walking, I kept going over things in my mind. Had I got things wrong? I was in such a fluster, I was halfway back before I realised that I had left my water pot at the well. It didn't seem to matter now, somehow. I seemed to have something far more satisfying than water inside me. As I went I began to figure it out. I had said that the Christ would tell us everything. I knew the stranger had told me everything that mattered – about myself and about God. He understood me, like no one else ever did. So I knew what he said was true – he was the Christ. He *is* the Christ!

As soon as people saw me, they realised something had happened. And when I spoke to them, they *knew* something had happened. I said, 'Come on! Come and meet a man who told me everything I ever did! Do you think he could be the Christ?' I put it that way, not because I was unsure myself, but because I realised they had to make up their own minds.

It was amazing. I thought I was only a few minutes rushing around telling everyone who would listen, but by the time I set off back across the fields, it looked as if the whole town was following me! And word was spreading like wildfire. As I looked back, people were leaving their work in the fields and it looked as if the fields were white with people streaming down to the stranger at the well.

He had hardly had time to get something to eat and to drink something from my water pot, but he didn't mind. He just sat there and answered people's questions. Everyone was so amazed and delighted that they asked him to stay, and he did – for two whole days.

At the end of that time, people were saying to me, 'At first we knew something amazing had happened to you. We could see the change. So we believed what you said about him. But now we have heard him for ourselves and we know that he really is the Saviour of the world.'

It felt great. From being an outcast, now I was someone that people wanted to come up to and thank. But what felt far better than that was that he understood me completely and yet loved me enough to speak to me, to show me myself and to reveal himself to me!

What do I say to people now? Just the same as I said to my neighbours then – the same as I say to you now. 'Come on! Come and meet a man who told me everything I ever did. Could he be the Christ? What do *you* think?'

# 5
# Big Forgiveness

Come on, let's go to Simon's place. You're new in town, and this would be just the thing to get to know people. Simon's throwing a party tonight. And Simon's really well off, he has a big house and he can throw a big party.

Tonight it's one of these open house affairs where there are specially invited guests to the banquet, but anyone can get in to the party and get something. Even the poor – the down-and-outs and beggars – can get in, as long as they behave themselves – as long as they sit quietly at the back, away from the table where the invited guests recline. People like Simon like to show off how charitable (and wealthy) they are. And believe me, Simon keeps a good table – plenty to eat and drink.

There's something else you'd better understand, before we go in. Simon's very religious. He belongs to one of these really strict organisations. It's a fundamentalist group. The Pharisees they're called

– very strict. So don't say anything out of place, all right? Don't speak to the guests at the table.

And another thing. Only men will be at the table – no women. Now, don't make a fuss about it – it's just a different culture, that's all.

Which reminds me, there's a little custom we have for welcoming guests. They get their feet washed, get some moisturiser on their faces and are greeted with a kiss. But not for us, I'm afraid. We're just the riff-raff.

Oh, and one last thing – there's a bit of excitement tonight. They're expecting a special guest – some sort of religious guru. No, not like Simon. In fact I'm surprised that Simon's invited him. There are all kinds of stories going around about him. Seemingly he's an amazing speaker. He gathers crowds wherever he goes. And he's some kind of faith-healer. But he doesn't please a lot of the religious people – like Simon. Doesn't keep up the standards. Mixes with the wrong kind of people – 'drunkards and sinners' (they're always calling people sinners). And he makes big claims for himself – claiming things they say are only true of God.

*What's he called?* Joshua. Although you may know him by his Greek name – Jesus, Jesus from Nazareth. All right, let's go in.

Right, there are the people getting their feet washed. Okay, now we're in. There's Simon, our host. Just bow to him, don't say anything. And there's the table. It's low – positively groaning with food. A lot of guests already reclining. Let's get a seat on the floor here beside this pillar, and have a look round. Nearly everyone is here. But no sign of Jesus. I wonder, is he going to come?

Everyone's gone really quiet. Wait a minute … there he is, just coming in. Yes, he's really quite ordinary looking, until he looks you in the eye, then … well, you'll see. Dear me, he's looking rather dusty and dishevelled. They can't have washed *his* feet, or anointed *him* – and he's not complaining. If it was one of these priests, they would kick up a real fuss! But he's just smiling and saying hello to people. Look, he's coming over to sit there in front of us.

You see what I mean? When he looks at you, it's as if he sees right through you. No, not right *through* you, but right *into* you … knows what you're thinking … makes you feel you should be a better person. Well, that's what I felt anyway. What did you feel?

Everyone's talking again now. Jesus is just sitting down. Look he's right opposite Simon. Did you see that little smile Simon gave to the person beside him? Looks like they think they're going to have some fun at Jesus' expense tonight.

I'd better be quiet now. Simon's getting up to make a speech and then they're going to serve the food.

Well, that was a rather good first course, don't you think? And everything's been very quiet so far.

Wait … what's everyone looking at? Oh no! Not her! That's all we need!

*Who is she?!* Can't you tell just by looking at her? The long hair uncovered, the heavy make-up. Well, it's usually heavy, but there's definitely something different about it tonight. Her mascara's running. She's been crying.

There's going to be a scene. Simon's going to have her thrown out. Wait a minute, she's coming over *here*. ... Do *you* know her? No? No, she's going straight to Jesus. She's going down on her knees right at Jesus' feet. There's definitely going to be a scene! This is really embarrassing.

She's not saying a word. She's just sobbing her heart out. Look at those tears! I never knew so much water could come out of anybody's eyes. She's made Jesus' feet all wet. Oh no! Now she's wiping his feet with her hair. And kissing them.

And here comes the perfume. That's expensive stuff! I wonder which of her clients gave her that?

And all the time Jesus is looking down at her. He's not angry. Not embarrassed. It's definitely a smile. But he looks sort of sad and kind at the same time.

Simon and all these religious people are not going to approve. They're going to make a real meal out of this. Look at the smile on Simon's face. Rather different from Jesus' smile. You can just tell what Simon's thinking. He wouldn't be seen dead letting a woman like that anywhere near him!

Now Jesus has turned to look straight at Simon. Did you see how the smile froze on Simon's face and he had to look away? Quiet now! Jesus is talking. I'd better translate for you.

'Simon, I want to tell you something.'

'What do you want to tell me?' asks Simon, who's looking distinctly uncomfortable.

You can hear a pin drop. Jesus is going to tell one of his famous stories.

'Two men owed money to a certain money-lender. One owed him £50,000, and the other £5,000. Neither of them had the money to pay him back, so he cancelled the debts of both. Now which of them will love him more?'

Simon is relaxed. This is easy! Money he knows about, although I'll warrant he's finding it difficult to get his head round the idea of cancelling such large debts!

'I suppose the one who had the bigger debt cancelled.'

Oh, Simon, don't you see? Jesus is setting you up!

Jesus says, 'You have judged correctly.' Now he turns and looks at the woman and says to Simon, 'Do you see this woman? I came into your house. You didn't give me any water for my feet, but she wet my feet with her tears and wiped them with her hair. You didn't give me a kiss, but this woman, from the time I entered, hasn't stopped kissing my feet. You didn't put oil on my head, but she has poured perfume on my feet!'

Simon is flushed – I don't know if it's with anger, embarrassment or perhaps a mixture of both. Boy! I wouldn't like to be in his shoes. ... But come to think of it, I feel I am in his shoes ... do you know what I mean?

Wait, Jesus is speaking again. This is the punch line.

'I tell you, her many sins have been forgiven – for she loved much. But he who has been forgiven little loves little.'

Then Jesus looks straight at the woman and says to her, 'Your sins are forgiven.'

Well! That really sets the cat among the pigeons. Everyone is starting to talk at once. But it's all variations on the same theme: 'Who is this who even forgives sins? Only God can forgive sins – and then only through a priest performing a ceremony. Who does he think he is?'

I don't know about you, but I think they're all missing the point somehow – launching into their religious arguments.

I'll never forget the look I saw on that woman's face just now, when Jesus said, 'Her many sins have been forgiven – for she loved much,' and 'Your sins *are* forgiven.'

She knew that Jesus understood. And I think *I'm* beginning to understand. She loves him, because it was from his lips she first heard that there's forgiveness for someone like her – big forgiveness – forgiveness that would wipe away every stain of her past life and make her clean again – forgiveness that only Jesus could give.

She knew she could never pay off her debt to God.

I suppose she still doesn't know how the debt can be cancelled, but she believes Jesus will take care of that. All she knows is that she loves him. That's why she did what she did tonight. She took the most precious thing she had – her perfume – and she used it to show how much she thought of Jesus. She was probably going to do it anyway, but when she saw how disrespectfully he was treated by Simon and the others, she wanted to show there was someone who loved him. And she just didn't care what other people thought of her.

But when it came to it, she was so overwhelmed with a sense of her own shame and unworthiness, she sobbed her heart out. She was so sorry. And yet Jesus accepted it all as the offering of a loving heart. Big sin, big forgiveness, big love.

Well, that's what I think anyway – I don't know about you.

But wait, the woman's leaving and Jesus is saying something else to her – 'Your faith has saved you; go in peace.'

Well, she certainly has faith in Jesus – to come in here in front of all these people and do what she did. He's no ordinary man and he prompts no ordinary reaction. Who *can* forgive sins, but God?

And see the look of peace on that woman's face! Her face is a mess, with all the crying and her make-up running and everything, but I'd give everything I had to have peace like that. I don't know about you – what do you think?

## The Prisoner

When I woke up that morning, it was the same. I'd always hated it when you live and grow and... I couldn't... hoping and waiting for a long time.

You might be wondering why I love this relationship. Well I don't know. That's just how it was. I don't... anymore. Everyone knew I was saying in a term, but at least it's not because I was lonely. I could talk to the dead and they didn't say anything back. In fact, they didn't say anything at all. I could say anything I liked and they didn't scold me, mock me, accuse me, criticise me or condemn me. They said nothing. I liked that.

I didn't have any friends. Well, there was Cohort, but he doesn't count. At least he didn't count. Then. He wasn't a friend. He was more an accomplice. I didn't even know his real name. I just called him Cohort, because he was smaller and weaker than me. After I'd given him a good beating, he knew his place. From

# 6
# The Price He Paid

When I woke up that morning, it was dark. I suppose it's always dark when you live in a tomb. But it just seemed darker that morning. And it had been getting darker for a long time.

You might be wondering why anyone would want to live in a tomb. Well I don't know why *anyone* would want to live in a tomb. I don't even know clearly why I was living in a tomb, but I think it was because I was lonely. I could talk to the dead, and they didn't say anything back. In fact, they didn't say anything at all. I could say anything I liked, and they didn't scold me, mock me, accuse me, criticise me or condemn me. They said nothing. I liked that.

I didn't have any friends. Well, there was Cohort, but he doesn't count. At least he didn't count then. He wasn't a friend. He was more an accomplice. I didn't even know his real name. I just called him Cohort, because he was smaller and weaker than me. After I'd given him a good beating, he knew his place. From then on, he said nothing as well. Whatever I did, he did. I liked that.

Why didn't I have any friends? It's a long story. I could start further back, but I suppose the best place to start is when I was seventeen. I was big and strong for my age and I worked on the family farm. Not long before that my father had been killed in a fight with one of the local hard men. But this guy was the son of the local big wheel. You know the type – big landowner, local politician. He had everyone in his pocket. So of course my father had started it. The son was only defending himself, etc., etc.

I wanted to go down there and break his neck. My mother pleaded with me to leave it. It would only cause worse trouble for us if I did anything. So I left it. But I didn't forget. It gnawed at me day and night. Sometimes when I was digging I saw his head under my spade, and I dug and slashed and dug and slashed until the sweat was pouring off me. Or when I was clearing stones off the land, as I threw these small boulders onto a cairn, I imagined I was throwing him there. Or when I was chopping wood, I saw his neck on the block.

I suppose nothing more would have come of it if they had left us alone. But of course they couldn't leave us alone – it just wasn't in their nature. And it wasn't in their scheme of things. They wanted our land. They ran this big pig farm and they were always wanting to expand. The earth itself isn't big enough for some people. The pressure was relentless. Things went from bad to worse, until one market day no one would buy our beasts. They were all too frightened. I remember this pig farmer and his son sneering at me as I took the beasts home again. And the son made some suggestive remark about my little sister. I stopped and turned and looked him right in the eye, but my mother grabbed my arm and dragged me away.

But that night my little sister never came home. I eventually found her lying in some bushes on the hillside that looks out over the sea. She had been strangled. And she had been interfered with.

There arose up within me a fury so great, it nearly overthrew my mind. But instead my heart turned to stone, and I was cold and deadly. With my staff in my hand I came down out of the darkened hills into the town, down the road to the inn. He was there outside the inn as I expected, drinking with his three henchmen. They saw me a fraction too late. They had just time to draw their long knives – knives that they had always found so effective in all their dirty work. But there is no knife in this world that could have withstood my wrath in that hour, or the long staff in my hand.

One fell never to rise again. One limped off howling into the inn. And the other ran off up the road to their farm screaming his head off. So none saw the end of their boss's son. And when they did see him again, none would recognise him.

I came to myself just in time. I saw the lights coming down from the farm and heard the many voices. I made for the hills.

I wasn't thinking straight. I should have gone home. I thought they would follow me, but by the time I realised they hadn't, it was too late. From the top of the hill I saw the flames rising from our house, and I heard the screams.

From that night I lost my mind. I wandered far over the hills, and many times the moon waxed and waned. How I survived I don't know. All I know is that day and night, sun and moon, darkness and light, a rage was growing in me that would destroy the whole world.

Then one day I saw a battle. I was hiding in some rocks on the hillside. And down below me on the plain a Roman legion was closing in on some rebel forces. I heard the noise – the tramp of feet, the clink of armour, the braying of trumpets. The Roman infantry closed ranks, creating an impenetrable shield wall. They advanced relentlessly and simply wiped out their enemies. I watched in horrified fascination. When the battle was over, I crept as near as I dared and saw them offering sacrifices of thanks to Caesar and Mars their god of war.

In that moment I knew exactly what I wanted. I called upon those powers. 'Enter me!' I said, 'Give me that power to wreak vengeance!' And right away I felt it. I could crush the mountains to dust and trample them under my feet. From that day I gave myself a new name – Legion – because inside me there was a power like the five thousand men of a Roman legion.

From then on it was a tale of destruction. When

that power was on me, nothing could stand in my way – no weapon, no bolted gate, no barred door. But it was a capricious power. Many the time it left me, and at the most inopportune moment. Several times I was in the midst of wreaking havoc on the pig farmer's property, when my powers abandoned me, leaving me to be chained and shackled and at the mercy of that ruthless man. If he had killed me right away, that would have been the end of me, but he just had to gloat. And the power came back on me with a vengeance, and the iron chains and shackles on my hands and feet cracked like clay pots, and all fled before my face.

I had no one left in the world that I cared for, or that cared for me. I lost all human dignity. I wore no clothes. When there was nothing else left to destroy, I turned on myself. I cut myself with stones. I knew this couldn't go on. Sooner or later I knew I was going to die. That's another reason I was attracted to the tombs. I knew that's where I was going, so I thought I might as well get there early.

Cohort lived there already, and once I'd put the fear of death in him, we put the fear of death into everyone else round there. No one bothered us there. And the caves of the tombs were our home. They were cut into the rocks of the hillside overlooking the sea.

It was quiet and dark in the tombs, but I had no peace. There were these voices in my head. They kept driving me on, relentlessly, like a Roman legion. Nothing could stand in their way – not even me. I was racked with guilt. The faces of my father and mother and sister would rise up before me, but nothing I had done would satisfy my vengeance, and I was driven into ever more desperate and brutal acts. I hated the world. I hated myself, and I wanted to destroy myself.

That morning the darkness was unbearable. In the night there had been a storm on the sea and the wind had been howling. But now it was deadly calm. I could stand it no longer. I rushed out of the cave, and Cohort followed me. Often I had gazed out into the depths of the sea, and that's where I was going. Maybe it was deep enough to drown the anger and the violence and the bitterness of my heart.

I was running to the high ground where the fields came right to the top of the cliffs at the edge of the sea. They were the fields of the pig farmer and they were full of pigs. It was appropriate somehow.

But I stopped dead in my tracks. In the little bay in front of me, a boat was coming into the shore. There were thirteen men in it, and as they stepped ashore, it was obvious that there was one of them of whom the others were clearly in awe. (I'll explain later why that was.)

I don't know what it was, but I felt this compulsion to run – and run towards him, not away from him. I ran right up to him and fell on my knees on the sand in front of him. He looked at me, and he didn't look angry or frightened or threatening. I was so far gone in evil and violence, I couldn't even recognise the expression on his face, but I knew there was no power on earth or in hell that could stand against him.

He spoke quietly, and he said, 'Come out of the man, you evil powers!' Something vaguely registered at the back of my mind, 'He called me a man, a human being!' It was a long time since anyone had called me that. But why? Why was he bothering with me?

I must have heard one of his friends say his name, because I heard myself screaming, 'Jesus, Son of God Most High, what do you want with me?' What I actually said was, 'What, you and me?' What I meant was: What have you got to do with me, what do we have in common, why are you interested in me?

Then the voices inside me started again and they were tearing me apart, and I screamed, 'Swear to God you won't torture me!' And I could hear Cohort just behind me squealing, 'Have you come to torture us before the time?' Poor Cohort and Legion! All we'd ever known was torture. We couldn't imagine anything else.

But Jesus was still looking at me. He was quite calm. He asked me quietly, 'What's your name?'

'Legion', I answered, and then the voices came out. 'For we are many,' they screamed, threatening like. But he just stood silent, and I could feel his power. Very soon the voices were gibbering and pleading, but they were using my voice. 'Don't send us away. Don't send us back to the Pit of Hell!' He remained as still as a rock, unmoved. They howled, 'At least send us into that herd of pigs!' That was the last time they ever used my voice.

Jesus turned and looked at the fields of pigs – a long slow look – then he took a deep breath. 'Go!' he said.

Everything happened at once. I felt – it's difficult to describe how I felt. The first thing I felt was relief, as if a great weight had been lifted off me. And I felt clean. Strange that, because I was still naked and filthy, but I *felt* clean. Something the same must have happened to Cohort, because he ran off shouting 'I'm clean! I'm clean!' It was the first time he'd spoken for years.

But I had no time to think about that, because everyone was looking over at the pigs. There were about two thousand of them and they were bunching together into a herd. They started to move. They were advancing towards us like an army. I think everyone was terrified they would pour down the slope and trample us – everyone except Jesus, that is. He stood unmoving and immovable. The herd of pigs wheeled away and went rushing down towards the cliffs, rank upon rank of them. Nothing could stop them. Rank after rank they plunged over the cliff into the sea and were drowned.

I knew then I was free. In a way, I felt sorry for those pigs, because that should have been me. It was me that should have been drowned in the depths of the sea, after all I had done. But I was free. And set free at such a cost! I turned to gaze at this man who was prepared to pay such a high price to set free a poor madman like me, and I thanked him over and over again. He just smiled and said the first thing I could do to show my gratitude was to wash in the sea and put some clothes on! We all laughed.

One of them, a big fisherman that they called 'The Rock' came to help me. As he helped me to scrub away the filth and clean my wounds, we talked. He asked me all about myself, and I asked him about Jesus.

'Who is he?' I asked, 'I know I called him the Son of God Most High, back there, but I don't know where those words came from. Who is he really?'

The big fisherman said it was strange – that was the very question they had been asking themselves in the boat. And he told me about the storm. They had been crossing the sea in the night and were caught in the storm. The boat was nearly sunk. They were terrified, but Jesus was sleeping peacefully in the stern of the boat. When they woke him, he stood up in the boat and said to the wind, 'Be quiet!' and to the waves, 'Be still!'

And the most amazing thing happened. That instant the wind dropped, and the sea was as smooth as glass. That was the thing that really astonished the big fisherman. The wind dropping could be a coincidence. But stormy waters don't suddenly turn as still as a pond. 'There is no power on earth that could do that,' he said. 'You were right to call him the Son of the Most High!'

A little while later, I was sitting there with them, clothed and in my right mind, when people started pouring down the hillside towards us. It seems the workers who had been looking after the pigs had rushed into town and told about the pigs. The word spread like wildfire, and people were coming from miles around to see what had happened.

As they gathered round, they were astonished to see me normal. They gazed in wonder at the empty field and then looked out to sea as if they were half expecting to see an army of pigs rise from the depths. But all the time their eyes kept coming back to Jesus. The pig-herds kept repeating what had happened and kept pointing at Jesus.

Then the pig farmer arrived and he pushed his way to the front with some of his henchmen. He was apoplectic with rage. He glared at me and he demanded, 'Who is responsible for this?' He was so angry and so out of breath, he could hardly speak. There was a silence, and Jesus said quietly, 'I am.' He stared at Jesus, half afraid in superstitious fear, half indignant at the outrage to his property.

'What is the meaning of this? I demand compensation. Do you know how much two thousand pigs are worth?'

'Yes, I know how much two thousand pigs are worth – none better', said Jesus, 'But it was a price worth paying.'

'Worth paying!' The pig farmer's eyes were nearly starting out of his head, 'Worth paying for what? And they weren't yours to pay with anyway, they're mine!'

'Did you create them?' asked Jesus, 'No. Then be not over-ready to claim ownership. They were the price I paid to set a man free.'

'A man!' the red-faced pig farmer exploded, 'A man! If you mean this lunatic, this murderer, this ... this nobody. ...' He jabbed his finger in my direction.

'Yes, a man', said Jesus. 'A man is worth more than two thousand pigs. I will pay a greater price yet to free such as this man. And here too is your compensation.'

The pig farmer looked around in enraged bewilderment.

'See, I have killed your enemy,' said Jesus, pointing at me, 'And I give him back to you as a friend!'

'A friend!' the man shrieked, his face turning deathly white, 'It'll be a cold day in...' But he never did say where it would be a cold day, because his mouth twitched, his body convulsed and he would have collapsed if his henchmen hadn't supported him. He glared at Jesus, and the last words anyone ever heard him say were, 'Get out of here!'

A great dread fell on the crowd and they all shrank back from us, and started pleading, 'Leave us. Please go.'

Jesus looked sadly at them all retreating back up the hillside, and then he turned and went down to the boat. All his friends went with him and I went too. I said, 'Please, I want to go with you. There's nothing here for me now.'

He looked at me, his face still sad. Then he smiled and said, 'Yes, there is something. There's something you must do for me here. And only you can do it. Go back to your own people and tell them how much the Lord has done for you, and how he has had mercy on you.'

'But, Jesus,' I said, 'I haven't got any people here now.'

His face became grave. 'I know,' he said, 'I know.' Then his face brightened again. '*They* are your people now.' He swept his arm over the hillside and the hastily retreating people.

It was the hardest thing I ever did, but I didn't get into that boat. I stood watching them sail out over the deep waters, and then I turned to the hills. I was going to tell everyone I met how much Jesus had done for me – and the price he paid.

# 7

# The Worst of Days and the Best of Days

It was the worst day of my life – and it was the best day of my life. It was the day I met him for the first time. I'd heard a lot about him of course – most of it not very complimentary, it must be said. Well, you don't know what to believe, really, do you? Or I didn't then.

He was certainly popular. People flocked from all over, just to hear him speak. The Preacher, they called him. He told stories. He explained about God. They said they'd never heard anything like it. It was powerful. They knew he meant every word.

Some people were saying he was anti-Semitic. They said they'd heard him say that God was more interested in the other nations than in the Jews. He said this in his home town synagogue. I'm a Jew myself – in fact a leader in the Synagogue – so I wasn't very encouraged by that.

But there were amazing stories going round about him. First off, there was healing. He was some sort of faith-healer. He even helped a Roman centurion – they said he healed his servant just with a word! But some people were saying it wasn't by God's power he healed – it was really by the devil. But the same people were saying he freed people from evil powers, so I couldn't make sense of that.

And another thing was this – he was always getting into trouble with the authorities over something or other. There was the famous occasion when a lot of our religious experts and theologians were there, and they actually heard him assure a man that all his sins were forgiven – like, all his sins – every sin he'd ever committed! I have that on good authority from people who were there. It's no wonder that they condemned him for blasphemy. Well, only God can do that, can't he? But there was a sting in the tail. The man was paralysed, right? And he told him to get up and walk – and he did! Of course, the man might not have been really paralysed – well, that's what I thought then – but now ... Well, anyway ...

He was always mixing with disreputable people as well. A friend of mine – well an acquaintance really, Simon – he told me about the time he invited him to his house for dinner and this woman came in. Everyone knew the kind of woman she was. She made a bee-line for Him and created quite a scene seemingly – weeping at his feet and everything. But he just accepted it and said she loved him so much because he had forgiven her so much. That didn't do his reputation much good with a lot of people. Well, to be perfectly honest, with me too. I did have my position to think about after all.

I suppose that would have been it really. I'm an ordinary sort of man. I don't like bother, and change, and controversy. And this man seemed to attract controversy wherever he went.

But it was my little girl. It all happened so fast. You know what kids are like. One day as right as rain and the next seriously ill ... and the next – well, she was at death's door. I don't know what it was. No one knew. They couldn't do anything for her.

I'd have done anything – she was my little girl. She was actually twelve years old, but she was still my little girl. I'd have done anything – I was desperate. I remember saying to my wife, 'I'd do anything'. And she looked at me. You know the way women look at you. And I knew. We both knew. There was only one person who could help us. And you know, suddenly all that stuff didn't matter anymore – all the things my colleagues said about him – my position in the synagogue. What did any of it matter now? I'd have walked over burning coals for her.

I went out to look for him. And at first the news wasn't good. He'd crossed over to the other side of the sea. Then I heard someone saying, 'The carpenter's back' – sort of sneering like. That's when I very nearly lost it. I caught him by his collar and said, 'What did you say?' I've never seen anyone look so frightened for a long time. I must have looked really wild. Anyway he told me that 'the blasphemer', as he called him, had just landed and there was a big crowd down at the harbour.

I fairly ran down the street and I pushed my way through the crowd. They just parted in front of me. I was the synagogue ruler after all. That's when I started to slow down. That's when I started to get frightened. Would he help me? I'd heard about how he'd given a hard time to people like me – old Nicodemus up in Jerusalem, for instance. And there were all these people. Maybe if he did help me, I'd be at the bottom of the list. Anyway it was all foolishness – it wasn't real, it wasn't true, it was all spin and exaggeration. I was going to throw away my reputation for that. I'd be a laughingstock.

I had actually stopped and I was just about to turn away, when two things happened. I saw my little girl lying on the bed, her face deathly white. And then I saw him. And I did something I'd never done before in my life. I went down flat on my face on the ground in front of him and I just said, 'My little girl is dying. Please come and lay your hands on her and heal her and she'll live.'

No sooner were the words out of my mouth than I felt this hand on me – a surprisingly strong hand, and then I remembered he was a carpenter. He caught me by the arm and lifted me to my feet. And he said, 'Come on, let's go!' I was never so relieved in all my life. I couldn't stop talking – telling him all about my little girl – as we made our way to my place.

The people kept crowding round us. Everyone wanted to ask him something or get him to do something. I don't know how he could stand it.

And then he just stopped and said, 'Who touched me?' Well, I thought he'd really lost the plot then. Who touched him? Who hadn't touched him? I didn't want to say it but, I mean, he was surrounded by a crowd! I didn't have to say anything, as it turned out, because his right hand man, Peter the big fisherman, said what everybody was thinking.

But he says, 'No, someone did touch me. I know because power went out from me.' And he kept looking around to see who it was.

By this stage I'm nearly frantic. We can't afford to waste time. My little girl is dying! Doesn't he care?

Then this woman came forward. She was really shaking. I recognised her. I'd had to exclude her from the synagogue. Women's troubles. I had no choice. The regulations were quite clear. Women suffering from bleeding had to be excluded. I was thinking, it's been a long time she's had that. It was round about the time my little girl was born … yes, twelve years ago. And I thought, she's had it 12 years. If she wants his help, can't she wait just a little bit longer till he sees my girl? She should get to the back of the queue!

And then she fell down at his feet. Just like I did a couple of minutes before. I suddenly felt differently about her. I'd been there. I knew how she felt.

But then something very strange happened. She wasn't asking for help. She explained who she was and what was wrong with her, how she had spent all her money on doctors who couldn't cure her. She said she came up behind him and just touched the edge of his cloak and she was instantly healed! You could see it in her face. Something had happened.

I didn't know whether to laugh or cry. I was happy for her, of course, but every moment was precious. There was no time to lose. My little girl was dying! Why was he delaying talking to her? She was already cured.

But he was really concerned for her and he told her that her faith had healed her, and she was free from her suffering.

I thought, 'Right, let's get on!' That's when it happened. I got hit right in the guts. I don't mean physically. That would have been nothing. Some of my men came from my house. They just shook their heads and said, 'Don't bother the Preacher any more. Your daughter's dead.' You know that empty feeling in the pit of your stomach. I was numb, completely numb. It was all for nothing. I'd been such a fool. She was gone. My little girl. All our hopes and dreams for her were all gone. And there was nothing anybody could do about it now.

That was when he looked me straight in the eye and said, 'Don't be afraid. Just believe. And she'll be fine!'

Now you might think that was the cruellest thing anybody could say to a father who'd just lost his little girl. But you weren't there. It melted my heart. You might say I was clutching at straws, and maybe I was. But he meant it. And I believed him.

When we got to the house, it was chaos. Everyone was in an awful state. All the aunties and cousins and neighbours were there and they were all howling.

When he could make himself heard, he said, 'Why all this noise? The girl isn't dead. She's just sleeping.' At that, hope rose up in me again, but it was quickly squashed. They all said, 'Rubbish. You don't know what you're talking about. We know a dead body when we see it!' That was the weirdest thing. People who a few seconds before were howling and crying their eyes out, were now laughing at him and mocking him. I was glad when he put them all out. And believe me, he put them out all right!

Then we went into my daughter's bedroom – my wife and I, and the three fishermen, Peter, James and John, and him. I think that was when all hope left me. She was dead.

But he just bent over her and took her by the hand. For a carpenter with big strong hands he did it so gently. He said, 'Get up, little girl!' Just like her mother used to say to her on a lovely summer morning when she'd overslept.

I've heard some people talking about miracles and they say this happened and then that happened and so on. It wasn't like that at all. No sooner had he said, 'Get up,' than she jumped out of bed! The colour came back to her face and she looked at him kind of funny and smiled. She walked over to her mum and me and – well, the rest is just a blur. I remember that he told us to give her something to eat. He'd raised the dead, but he wasn't going to feed the hungry, at least not that day!

He said a funny thing then. 'Don't tell anyone about this!' He was really serious about that. I thought, 'Some hope!' A lot of people had seen her dead, and a lot of people were going to see her alive. But it was so like him. Some people said he was a self-publicist – always promoting himself. But that's not true. He did the most amazing thing ever. He raised the dead – and then he told us to keep quiet about it! It's like he did those things just because he loved people, even people like me who didn't deserve it. He didn't want people to be mesmerised by his powers, he wanted them to be captivated by his love. At least that's what I think. You'll have to make up your own mind. And you'll *have* to make up your own mind now, won't you?

Who was he? You know who he was. Jesus, Jesus of Nazareth. I'll never forget the day he came into my life – the worst of days and the best of days.

# 8

# The Highest Mountain

It was the day that changed my life. The day I climbed the highest mountain – Mount Hermon, over 9000 feet.

Now, I'm not a mountaineer – more of a seaman myself. Give me a boat with a wind in the sails and the waves rolling under it, or even a dead calm and the tug of the living waters under the oars. But my friend loved the mountains. He was always dragging us up hills! And I came to love them too. He had that kind of effect on you. I call him my friend. He was that, but much more than that, and it was that day that I really grasped how much more.

Up until I met him I'd lived around the Sea of Galilee – occasional visits to Jerusalem, but not much more. And he was much the same. I only got to know him in the last three years of his life – but what years they were! I could tell you about a night on the sea – one of the roughest I ever saw – and since then I've seen mighty storms on the Great Sea and I've heard about ones beyond the Pillars of Hercules. But I want to tell you about the mountain.

This day he decided to leave Galilee and we travelled north. We were all there – my brother Andrew, and my friend John and his brother James (we'd been fishermen together), and eight others. We all thought it was a strange place for him to want to go to – Caesarea Philippi it was called at that time. Philip, one of King Herod's family, had rebuilt the city in honour of Caesar, the emperor. It was a really pagan place – Greeks, Romans. You should have seen the buildings – the temples and the idols. The place used to be called Paneas, after the Greek god Pan, the god of nature.

We were all a bit scared – it was creepy. But not him! At the time it seemed a strange place for him to want to visit. I've got used to such things now. I've been in many cities. I've been to Rome! And I think I understand now – why he took us there, but it did seem strange at the time.

The mountain? Yes, the mountain. You could see it from there, all right. Its snow-capped peaks dominate that whole area. In fact you can see it from around the Dead Sea, a hundred and twenty miles away.

Yes, the mountain. But first we stopped at a little place a bit nearer. That's when he asked us. 'Who do people say I am?' Just straight out. No beating about the bush. That was always his way. Of course that was easy to answer. Because people had to have an opinion about him – the things he did ... and said.

'Elijah,' we said. 'Some people say you must be Elijah, the power you have.' Yes, Elijah was a mountain man too. It was on Mount Carmel he defeated the pagan priests.

Some said, 'Jeremiah or one of the prophets', or 'John the Baptiser'. John was actually his relative. Like, but unlike. John had power all right – before Herod stuck him in prison, and then had him beheaded. He was a powerful preacher. That's when I first met *him*. We'd gone to hear John preach. And boy, he could preach! But *he* was there. Andrew it was who introduced me to him. And he said a strange thing to me. He said I would be known by a different name – the Rock. I discovered it's the kind of name you have to grow into!

But the mountain. Yes. That was rock all right! I felt very small looking up at it.

But I felt very big when I answered his next question. 'But what about you? Who do you say I am?' He put you right on the spot – always! Not that I minded that then. Full of self-confidence in those days I was. The others must have hesitated. Maybe it was the mention of John the Baptist and the memory of what they had done to him.

'The Messiah', I said, 'The Son of the living God!' No half measures! I was big and bold then – not bent and old like I am now – and I didn't care who heard me. Because I believed it. Maybe I didn't understand it – not like I understand it now. But sure, I believed it.

You don't see a man standing up in boat out at sea in a Force ten gale and telling the storm to stop, and it does, and think 'O, that happens all the time!' Get real! I may not know the mountains, but I know the sea. That just doesn't happen. But it did. That's the point.

Anyway – to get back to my story – it was what he said next that amazed me. He called me "The Rock," and then he said he would build his people on the rock and the gates of Hell would not conquer them. And he said he would give me the keys of his Kingdom.

Well, I felt kind of embarrassed, but I must confess I felt proud too – very proud. Too proud, as it turned out. I didn't understand then that it was my faith in *him* that was the real rock. It was only that that gave me, or anyone else, the right to open the door of his Kingdom to anyone, or to close it against those who would not believe in him.

They say pride goes before a fall. It was certainly true in my case. Because he went on to teach us about what was going to happen in Jerusalem. We didn't know what he was talking about then, but actually he was telling us exactly what was going to happen – what did happen – that the religious powers-that-be were going to turn on him and get him put to death. But that was not going to be the end – three days later he would be back.

I really thought he was losing it – we all did. But it was Big Mouth here who had to say it. 'Never!' I said, 'That's not going to happen!' I didn't understand then. I thought – we all did – that the Messiah was going to rule a powerful kingdom, like his ancestor the great King David. Set us free. Put everything to right. End the oppression. Well, yes, he did all that – but not in the way we expected. It wasn't the Romans we needed to be freed from. We were enslaved on the inside.

He turned on me like a flash. And his words still make my blood run cold. 'Get out of my sight, Satan!' Yes, he even called me that. That hurt! 'You want to bring me down,' he said, 'It's human ideas you have in mind, not God's. What good is it if you gain the whole world, yet lose your soul?' I was hurt and confused. But I know now he was right. I'm glad he's not now sitting on Herod's throne with a gold crown on his head. I'm glad he didn't turn aside from that cruel wooden throne and that crown of thorns. He bore our sins in his own body on the tree. By his wounds we are healed.

I know that now, but then I thought you could gain the whole world, keep in with the world, and keep your soul. It can't be done. I know.

But the mountain. Yes, the mountain. It was just the four of us. He took me and my two friends, the brothers James and John. Just the four of us – we set out in the early morning. The mist was still down. There was a heavy dew on the ground. Then as we went up, the mist started to clear and we could see the top – still a long way off, the snow on the top glistening in the sun.

I wasn't really built for the mountains. Didn't really have the legs for it. More upper body strength. All that pulling on the oars and hauling in the nets. I was fairly gasping for breath by the time we reached the first high ridge. I'd never been so high. I'd climbed the hills round Galilee of course – nothing like this. But it was marvellous. You could see for miles. By the time we were near the top we could see Galilee and the Jordan valley. We thought we could even see the Dead Sea, away on the edge of sight. What a day!

It was like being in another world – dreamlike, but not unreal – somehow more real. The snow was dazzlingly white in the sun, whiter than anything I'd ever seen. It was cold too, and you couldn't seem to get enough air. The three of us were getting quite sleepy in fact.

He started to pray. He often prayed in the hills, away from all the crowds – in the peace and quiet, surrounded by God's handiwork, not man's.

That's when it happened. At first I didn't know what was going on. My eyes were closed. To tell you the truth, I might have dozed off. But something made me open my eyes, and when I did, I saw this light falling on James and John. It seemed to be coming from behind me. It seemed all wrong. The sun was still high in the sky but in front of me. This light was coming from the opposite direction – and very bright. And the look on John's face. That's what really made me turn round.

I'll never forget what I saw. It was him all right, but not as I'd ever seen him before. I'd seen his power – when he healed a paralysed man, or when he brought a dead girl back to life. And I'd seen his majesty – when he walked on the Sea of Galilee in the middle of a raging storm, or when he walked through a hostile crowd and they parted before him like the waves before the prow of a ship. I'd seen him angry – when he looked round at the hypocritical Pharisees who would rescue their beasts on the Sabbath, but criticised him for healing a man. And I'd seen that look of love in his face, when he saw the crowds harassed and helpless, like sheep without a shepherd, or when he said to that woman, 'Your sins are forgiven.'

But this was different. It was all these rolled into one – and more. There was glory. There was brightness so bright you couldn't look at it, but you couldn't look away either. It was as if you were really seeing for the first time.

At first I didn't see the other two, such was his splendour. But then I realised he was speaking to two others, nearly – but no, not quite – as glorious as himself. I heard him call one of them Moses and the other Elijah. Moses! Moses who had received the Law from the hand of God on the top of Mount Sinai far to the South, and who had died on the top of another mountain, Mount Nebo on the border of the Promised Land.

And Elijah! Elijah who had faced down the pagan priests on Mount Carmel, out there to the west, and who was taken up to heaven in a chariot of fire. Moses and Elijah! There were mountain men if you like!

People have often asked me what they were talking about. We didn't properly understand – at least not then. I thought they were talking about the exodus at first – the exodus out of Egypt – because that's the word they used, exodus – when God redeemed his people from the slavery of Egypt. But they were talking about a greater redemption, the one Jesus was going to achieve on a hill much smaller than Hermon. A brutal place – a hill called the Skull, outside Jerusalem – where he died for the sins of the world. It just goes to show, it's not how big or how high a place is that matters – or a person.

Moses and Elijah were just about to leave, when I said it. I just blurted out, 'Lord, it's good for us to be here! Let me put up three shelters – one for you, one for Moses and one for Elijah.' I don't know what got into me. I think I was terrified. I didn't know what I was saying. I just didn't want that moment to end, and I kind of thought, 'Here are the three greatest men who have ever lived.'

The words weren't out of my mouth, when we were enveloped in this cloud – it was a cloud, but it was bright. It shone.

And then this voice came from the cloud. I could hear and understand every word. But that voice came from no human throat. It was the voice of God I heard that day.

'This is my Son whom I love. With him I am well pleased. Listen to him!'

We all fell flat on our faces in sheer terror. Then I

felt this hand on my shoulder. I nearly died. But when I looked up, it was Jesus. The same Jesus we knew and loved. But from that day on, I never thought of him in exactly the same way ever again. I now knew the meaning of the words I'd spoken so thoughtlessly – 'the Son of the living God'.

It was the day that changed my life – that day on the highest mountain.

# 9
# The Road Not Taken

You know how sometimes you look back at a particular time in your life and wonder what would have happened, if you'd done something different, taken a different road.

Well, I sometimes feel like that – not very often, but sometimes – like now. I don't know why, but every so often it all comes back to me – that day. Perhaps it's just when I'm feeling a bit down. Things haven't worked out – and I feel things might have been different. Or maybe it's just that I can't get him out of my mind. I don't know.

I was young then, full of all the idealism of youth. You know – believing you could find an answer to every question, believing in human goodness, believing you could get the key to eternal happiness!

I was religious too. Still am, I suppose. Only now I'm not so idealistic – more going through the motions, really. Lost the zeal of youth, the certainty, the commitment. I'm still a leader in my community, of course, but somehow it's not the same – never has been since that day.

I suppose life is ... well ... satisfactory, comfortable. I'm well off. Comfortably well off, some would say. I have my things. A place for everything and everything in its place. My parents taught me possessions were important. They showed a man's status – and not just among men. We believed – well everybody did then – that if you were well off, it showed God's favour. I don't know if I believe that any more – I'm not sure what I believe. But I don't seem to have God's favour. I'm still well off. But happy? I don't know. Comfortable, but not comforted. Satisfactory, but not satisfied.

Maybe these are just the thoughts of a jaded old man. Perhaps if I go and look at that new plot of ground I've bought and the plans for my new house, that will cheer me up.

But I've tried that often enough. Takes my mind off things for a time. But then memory is a strange thing. Just when you're least expecting it. Wham! Back it comes – the memory of that day. And the look on his face.

I suppose I should start at the beginning. As I say, I was young. I'd been well brought up. I followed all the rules. And believe me there were a lot of rules. But I liked that ... still do. It gives a kind of sense of security – a rule for everything and everything by a rule.

But then at that stage of my life – you know, when you start asking questions – I felt there must be more, more to life than following a set of rules. It somehow didn't satisfy. I could never be sure I was keeping all the rules. I thought I was, but there seemed to be something missing.

It all came to a head about one thing really, one thing I wasn't sure about – death and dying and what happens then. I know. When you're young you think a lot about death; then when you're old and death is a lot nearer, you don't want to think about it. I know. Well, that's not totally true. I do think about death still, and I'm no nearer knowing the truth.

Back then, there was a lot of talk about eternal life – living forever – getting to heaven. They say the young think they're immortal. But that's wrong. We all know we're going to die – sooner or later. And then what?

People said to me, 'Oh, you'll be all right! You've never done anything wrong. God will be only too pleased to have you in his heaven!' But I wasn't so sure. Something was missing. Maybe I hadn't done bad things. But had I done enough good things? How could you be sure?

Anyway, that's when I heard about him. He was – well, I don't know what you would call him. A guru, or a prophet perhaps. We called him a Rabbi, a teacher. The Teacher, some called him. I'm not sure, in light of all that happened, that was right. But that's what he was called anyway. That's what I called him that day – the time I went to see him and to ask him my question.

Why did I go to see him? I'd heard a lot about him of course; who hadn't? People said all sorts of things about him – wild things – both for him and against him. But there were two things that impressed me about him. He was good and he was a teacher. That's what I called him that day – Good Teacher.

He was an amazing teacher. People came from all around just to hear him. He spoke with authority – not like a lot of the religious teachers. They talked about this authority and that authority. This interpretation and that interpretation. He just told it straight. Told stories too. Even the children enjoyed that. In fact that day when I ran up (yes, I know, I was running – I'll tell you about that in a minute) – that day he was surrounded by little children. He was saying something like, 'God's kingdom belongs to little children.' I never really understood what he meant.

That was the thing, you see. You wanted to believe what he was saying, but you couldn't quite understand it. Well, some people claimed to understand, but I'm not sure they did.

But you did want to believe him. That's because he was good. 'Good Teacher.' I don't just mean he was good at teaching. He was a good person. He made time for people. He answered their questions. He loved people. He showed compassion to the poor, the blind, the beggars, and the lepers – the disabled, the disinherited and the disreputable.

So I thought he might help me. I didn't need charity. I just needed to have my question answered.

I've often wondered since why I put it the way I did: 'What good thing must I do to inherit eternal life?' I suppose it was because my father had recently died. I was thinking about all I'd inherited from him. I've still got a lot of his things. Of course I've added a lot of my own now. Anyway, I was thinking about that and of course I was thinking about death, and wondering if he was happy now, and wondering how I could have eternal life. Was it something you could inherit? Or was there something you had to do?

Now, you may have heard bits of my story before. There were a few versions of it going around for a while. I'm not saying any of them were wrong, but I'll try to tell you the whole story like it happened.

He was visiting our town. He was on his way to Jericho. And there was some talk about him not coming back. I'd often intended to speak to him, but had never really got round to it – you know the way it is. But that day something compelled me. I don't know – did I have a premonition, or what? He never did come back.

Anyway, that's why I was running. I was frightened I'd miss him. I wanted to ask him my question. I came running up and fell down on my knees. It's the kind of impetuous gesture you make when you're young. I couldn't do it now. I don't think my knees could bend that far!

I blurted out my question. And he looked at me. I didn't feel stupid or anything. I was the only person in the world as far as he was concerned and my question was the only question. At least that's the way I felt.

Then he caught me off guard. He came back at me with a question. Two really. 'Why do you ask me about what's good? And why do you call me good?' I was just about to say, 'Because you're good!' when he said, 'No one's good but God alone.'

That really made me think! What was he saying? Was he saying he wasn't good? Or was he saying he was God? But he couldn't have meant that, surely?

Then he said if I wanted to get to heaven, I should keep the commandments. 'Which ones?' I asked, because there were hundreds of rules. He said, 'Do not murder. Do not commit adultery. Do not steal. Do not testify falsely. Honour your father and mother. Love your neighbour as yourself.'

To tell you the truth, I was a little disappointed. I'd expected something new. The Ten Commandments! I'd learned them with my mother's milk. And of course I'd kept them. Never killed anyone, or gone off with someone else's wife, or any of that stuff. People in my area were all good living, well off people. So of course I was a good neighbour too.

Or that's what I thought then. It was only later I noticed that he had missed out quite a lot. He'd missed out the first four commands – about loving and worshipping God – and the last one, the one about coveting. I was quite glad he'd missed that one. I'd never really seen the point in it. It wasn't as if just *thinking* something was going to harm anyone, was it?

But there was a sting in the tail. I said, 'I've kept all these since I was a child. But there's still something missing. What is it?'

He said, 'Sell all you have and give the money to the poor, and you will have treasure in heaven. Then come, follow me.'

That really knocked me sideways! I wasn't expecting that. I mean, it was completely unreasonable! My father had built up that wealth, and his father before him. It was wrong to ask me to squander it all on those down and outs and drop-outs. They should earn their living. Do a proper day's work, instead of begging!

I still think it was unreasonable. But, you know, it hurt. Not so much what he said – but walking away. Because that's what I did. I walked away. But it hurt. It still does. You know why? Because of the way he looked at me when he said, 'Come, follow me.'

No one's ever looked at me like that. Not my father or mother, not my best friend, not my wife, not even my children. It was pure love. I don't know how else to describe it. That look said, 'You're the most precious person in the world to me. Leave behind those cheap worthless things and come with me on the road to glory!' And you know, I almost did something very stupid then. I almost believed him, I almost gave in.

But it was utterly unreasonable what he was asking. If he'd asked anything else, I'd have done it. I'd have fasted and given up drinking wine. I'd have left my wife. I'd have attended synagogue seven days a week. But he had no right to ask me to give up my things.

So that's why I went away sad. I wanted to follow him. I wanted to be with him. It would have been exciting. But it was out of the question. He was asking too high a price.

As it turns out, it was just as well I remained sensible that day. Just a short time later, we heard what happened to him. He was in the capital and the authorities arrested him. Seemingly he had got on the wrong side of some very powerful people. He was interrogated of course. Reported to the Governor. I've heard the Governor thought he was innocent. But there were some strange goings on. In the end he was condemned. A public execution. I was in town at the time and people asked me if I wanted to go. I'm glad I didn't. He was a sorry spectacle. It's a gruesome business. But by all accounts he died well. Perhaps he knew where he was going.

A good thing that – to know where you're going. Do I know where I'm going? To be perfectly honest, no. I took a different road that day. I sometimes wonder about the road not taken. Am I happy? Well, I'm comfortable. Life is ... satisfactory. I have my things.

# 10
# The Lost Rescued

It was a long weary day, just like every other day for so long I can't remember. They took me to the same place on the same street as they had for as many days as I can remember. They settled me down and made me as comfortable as they could.

I had a good pitch. It was a busy street, the main road into town – and it was a very busy town. A lot of people passed that way – which was good for business. Not much of a business, you might say, just sitting there in the dark waiting – waiting for someone to pay me.

What was I selling? I was selling happiness! They gave me money, and they felt happier. They came along the street and they saw me, and they felt guilty. They gave me some money and then they felt better! At least that was true for most of them, I guess. There were some, who were happy already. They always had a quiet word and made you feel less disgruntled with yourself and with the whole sorry business.

There were others, the most religious ones – you could usually tell when they came by. Either you heard them a mile off at some street corner praying their heads off, or everything went very quiet when they came past. And they made sure everybody knew they were giving you some money – and how much it was. I've never known people with such loud voices!

Of course there were people who completely ignored you. There were the officials and the military people hurrying past with great pomp and ceremony.

I suppose there was one great advantage in being where I was and doing what I did. I heard all the news – better than being stuck at home. There wasn't much going on in Jericho that I didn't know about – who was up to no good, who was cheating who.

That was one thing to be thankful for, I suppose. There was nothing wrong with my hearing. I could tell a great deal about what was going on around me. It's funny how some people think if you can't see, you can't hear either! I overheard a lot of conversations – some that the people talking would have preferred no one had heard. But usually it was only a disjointed snatch of conversation as they passed by: 'Did you hear the latest ...?' Or, 'Do you know what she said then?' And I never did hear the latest, or know what she said next. But I learned a lot.

One thing interested me greatly. There was a lot of conversation about one particular man who was causing quite a stir throughout the country and in the capital. Seemingly the top people wanted rid of him. Not that that surprised me – not from what I'd heard of some of the 'top people'. Two of them once came on a man who'd been robbed and badly beaten. This was on the main road down here from the city. These 'top people' left him to die. It was a foreigner, a stranger in these parts, in fact one of the hated Samaritans, who actually helped him.

Anyway, this man I was telling you about, he used to tell that story, and some people didn't like it seemingly. It was not patriotic, or religiously correct. Not that he bothered with being religiously correct, from all accounts.

But that's not what interested me. What interested me was – well two things really. The first was that although he came from a place in Galilee, a town called Nazareth, there was a story going round that he really belonged to Bethlehem and was descended from King David. I've always had a soft spot for King David – especially that story about him showing kindness to that lame man, the grandson of his enemy King Saul. Seemingly his descendant was the same.

That's the second thing that interested me about him – he was kind to people like me. But not just kind like some other people were kind. He actually did something about it. I'd heard stories that he'd made the lame walk, the deaf hear and even the blind see. Some said that this proved he was The Descendant of David, The Son of David, the One all the prophets had foretold. That interested me very much!

Then one day I met him. I might have missed him that day. If I had, I'd never have met him or got his help. Because that was the last time he visited Jericho – he was just passing through really, on his way up to Jerusalem for the last time.

I very nearly didn't meet him. Oh, I was in my usual place, all right, from early on. Then out of the blue this crowd started passing by. I knew something big was going on, but I couldn't make out what it was. I never liked crowds. Not only did people trip over you and curse you, not only were you nearly choked with all the dust, but you never knew what was going on – all the noise and bustle – you couldn't hear properly. No one took any notice of a blind beggar by the side of the road. I never felt more alone, more lost really, than in the middle of a crowd.

But this day some people did take notice, perhaps because I was bellowing so loud, when I asked what was going on. They said, 'It's Jesus. It's the man from Nazareth. Jesus is coming through. He's just passing by now!'

That's when I let out a roar. I don't know where it came from really, that voice. It seemed to come from the tip of my toes up through my belly, into my chest and when it came out it was like a trumpet! It think it was the suddenness of it all. I knew it was now or never.

'Jesus, Son of David,' I roared, 'Help me for pity's sake!'

Then I heard all these voices. Some officious, 'Keep quiet. We don't want a scene. We don't want him doing one of his "miracles" here!' Some sneering, 'He's not going to be interested in you, Bartimaeus. We all know you must have done something bad to be made blind.'

That's when something inside me snapped. I knew I'd done bad things. And maybe I did deserve to be blind, but they didn't have to say it. That was cruel. From all I'd heard, Jesus was not like that. So I yelled even louder. Only now my voice was cracked – it sounded like an old raven croaking. 'Son of David,' I croaked,' Have mercy on me!'

The next thing I knew, people were saying, 'Okay, you can stop bawling now! Cheer up! On your feet! He wants to see you, after all!' I threw aside my cloak with all my takings, and with some help I groped my way towards his voice.

It was a strong voice, but kindly – although the first thing he said took me aback. He asked me, 'What do you want me to do for you?'

What did I want him to do for me! Wasn't it obvious? But then I thought, 'He's offering me anything! What do I really want? Do I want loads of money? Do I want fancy clothes? Do I want people to treat me with respect? Do I want to marry a nice girl?'

Sure, all these things would be nice. But are they

what I really need? I'm in the darkness. I'm confused. I'm lost. I'm blind!

'Lord,' I said, 'I want to see!'

I thought there might be some discussion then, but no! He just said, 'Receive your sight!' And then he added, 'Your faith has healed you!' Now, I'd heard about another blind man he'd healed and it was a gradual process. But not me! No sooner were the words out of his mouth than I was looking straight at his face. I remember thinking kindness just shone from his face. Then I looked from one side to the other, and I nearly fell over! There was a riot of brightness and colour and shapes all around. I felt dizzy. I'd forgotten how bright the world was! It took some getting used to again.

But Jesus was on the move and I went with him, telling everyone who would listen how great God was in sending Jesus to help poor people like me.

Jesus wanted to know all about Jericho – what was happening, what was wrong with the place. Well, I told him all about the uneven roads and people putting all these obstacles out on the streets – shopkeepers' stalls, signs and things like that. He just smiled and said that maybe I could do something about that now that I could see.

I told him about the taxes too, of course. They say there's two things certain in life – death and taxes! Well, taxes were certain in Jericho, and lots of them! Everyone complained about them. Even the poor were taxed. The tax collectors said, 'Don't blame us.' They had to collect enough to make a living themselves and pass on enough for the chief inspector of taxes to pay the Romans and make a tidy profit himself. There were all kinds of scams and rip-offs going on.

'Who is he?' Jesus asked, 'Who is this chief tax inspector?' Well, that was easy, everyone knew that. Zacchaeus. That was his name. 'You'll easily know him,' I said, 'They say he's the smallest man in Jericho. Smallest man with the biggest house!'

It was just shortly after that Jesus stopped. He was looking up into a tree. I was still getting used to having my sight again, and at first I couldn't make out what was going on. Then I saw. There was this person perched up in the branches like a bird. He was hot and flustered and looking rather embarrassed, because people were pointing and laughing.

Then Jesus called him by name. He called him Zacchaeus! So that was Zacchaeus! No wonder people were laughing. I actually felt sorry for him, though, because he had obviously got up there so he could see Jesus passing by. And I knew what it was like to be laughed at. He must have wanted to see Jesus pretty bad to have risked people's ridicule.

'Zacchaeus,' Jesus was saying, 'Come down immediately. I must stay at your house today!'

Zacchaeus was delighted. His whole face lit up and you could tell by his voice he was amazed. He clambered down and led Jesus off to his house, with me and a few others in tow.

Not everyone, mind you. There were some who

were muttering things. They didn't say it out loud to Jesus' face. But my hearing was excellent. I was used to hearing things that people whispered. They were sneering, 'He's gone to be the guest of a sinner!'

You see, these religious people thought that tax collectors like Zacchaeus were bad, not really because he cheated (they were pretty good at that themselves), but because he mixed with unclean foreigners – the Romans. They thought the same about beggars like me, the blind and the lame – we were unclean. And of course prostitutes and people like that – we were all the same in their eyes.

They probably didn't say all this out loud, because they were frightened of being on the receiving end of one of his stories. Like another time when some of the religious leaders had criticised him for eating with 'tax collectors and sinners', he told three stories – about the lost sheep, the lost coin and the lost son. I liked the one about the lost son especially. It goes something like this.

*There was this man who had two sons. And the younger son asked his father to give him his share of the inheritance right away. So the father divided up all his property between the two of them. But the younger son went off with his share to a country far away and wasted the lot there. When he lost everything, there was a famine. But all his fair-weather friends were gone. Nobody wants to know you when you're down and out! He got a job feeding pigs and he was so hungry he wanted to eat the pig-swill.*

*It was there in that far country in filth and squalor that he came to his senses. He remembered his home. Even his father's casual labourers were well provided for, and here he was, starving to death. He realised he'd gone far wrong. He'd hurt his father and done bad things. He decided he would go back home and confess what he'd done. He realised he could no longer be considered a son; he just wanted to be treated like one of his Father's hired men.*

*It was a long way back. But eventually he was near home. He was skin and bone and he smelt something terrible. But while he was still a good distance away, he saw his father running to meet him. His father threw his arms around him and kissed him and said, 'Welcome home, son!'*

*But the son said, 'Father, I've hurt you and I'm a filthy sinner. I don't deserve to be called your son.'*

*But his father said, 'You're my son. You're back from the dead. You're going to get cleaned up and dressed, and we're going to have a welcome home party!'*

*Well the party was in full swing, with music and dancing, when the older brother came home from work. He was not well-pleased! In fact, when he heard his brother was welcomed home, he refused to go into the house.*

*His father come out and pleaded with him to go in. But he would have none of it. He said that he'd been slaving away for his father all these years, and lived a good life and did what he was told. But his father had never even given him a special meal. 'And when this fellow who was a waste of space comes home,' he said, 'this fellow who squandered your money on prostitutes, you throw a party for him!'*

*His father said, 'I already gave you everything, my son. It's all yours! You don't have to ask permission to have a party! But your brother was dead and he's alive again. He was lost and now he's found!'*

I love that story! And that's what happened that day at Zacchaeus's house. The dead came alive, the lost were found. Zacchaeus was a changed man. After the meal, he stood up and said to Jesus, 'I have all the wealth anyone could ever need, but I wasn't happy. I knew I was wrong. Something was missing. That's why I climbed up that tree today. I'd heard about you, and I was desperate to meet you, because I didn't know I'd have another chance. I'd heard that you would help even people like me. You have. You've rescued me. And so I want to do something good for a change. I want to show the love you've shown to me. I'm going to give away half of my wealth to the poor and needy. I'm going to stop cheating, and those I have cheated, I'm going to repay four times the amount I owe them.'

Well, we were gob-smacked! Never had anything like this happened in Jericho – certainly not to a tax-collector! Jericho would never be the same again. Jesus had walked into Jericho and not only had he changed my life. He'd changed the whole town, because he changed Zacchaeus.

The last thing I remember about that evening was something Jesus said. 'The Son of Man,' he said (that was the particularly humble title he gave himself), 'The Son of Man has come for this very reason – to search for and rescue the lost.'

And that's what we were – Zacchaeus and I, in our different ways – lost. Just like the younger son, perhaps just like you. Do just what I did. Jesus was passing by, never to pass that way again. Just cry out, 'Jesus take pity on me!' and he will.

# 11
# The Moon to Blood

I can remember it all as clear as if it was just yesterday – in fact clearer than yesterday. That day will always be etched on my memory – the day the sun turned to darkness and the night the moon turned to blood.

I was his friend – his best friend. He had three close friends: Simon, my brother James and me.

It's difficult to know where to start. I could start a week before, or even three years before. But really it all came to a head the night before.

We were meeting, the four of us and the other nine, in an upstairs room we'd booked especially for the celebration. Every year we had that celebration, remembering the time our people had been set free from slavery – slavery in the most powerful nation on the face of the earth. I'd done it many times before; but there was never a night like that – and never will be again.

We'd always thought we were looking back: looking back to that night when the Angel of Death passed through the land to kill every firstborn – that night when the blood of a lamb smeared on the door-frames of the houses of the slaves was their only protection and their redemption – that night when the mightiest nation on earth was brought down and the slaves went free.

We never thought that we should have been looking forward, looking forward to God doing a new thing – the redemption not of one people only, but of the world. The greatest thing that has ever been done. And that night, that greatest thing was only hours away.

We didn't know that then, when my friend took the cup of wine and told us all to drink it. He said, 'This is my blood – the blood of a New Covenant – poured out for the forgiveness of many people.' He'd said things like that before. He'd once said, 'Whoever eats my flesh and drinks my blood has eternal life!' We hadn't a clue what he meant.

But tonight was different, because things were coming to a head. All that talk about his blood gave me a bad feeling. We were meeting in secret, because we knew the authorities were out to get him. He'd offended them by telling the truth – by exposing their corruption and their ignorance. We knew he was in danger, and we wanted to protect him. Simon had a blade and one of the others had one too.

Then he dropped the bombshell. He said one of us was going to betray him. We were all stunned. We were hurt and confused. But Simon secretly asked me to find out who he meant, and it was Judas, but before anyone knew what was happening he'd left. It was night by then and Judas went out into the darkness. I never saw him again but once. It was only later we understood what had been going on. He had another god – money. He looked after all the donations for the poor and he helped himself. Simon would have throttled him if he'd known! Anyway, Judas could see which way the wind was blowing. He wasn't going to make a fortune as Chancellor of this new kingdom of tramps and beggars, and women who wasted expensive ointment by pouring it on Jesus's head! So he cut his losses and sold him, for just four months' wages – blood money.

After Judas left, Jesus – yes, that's who my friend was – he had a lot to tell us. I wrote most of it down eventually. But one thing kept recurring. He said, 'I'm leaving.' He said it in a dozen different ways. But one thing stuck in my brain. He was telling us we had to love each other, and he said, 'No one has a greater love than this: to lay down his life for his friends.' Then he said, 'You are my friends.' I think I knew then, though I didn't want to admit it to myself.

It was the middle of the night when we left the city. Down into the Kidron valley and up the other side to an olive grove. A friend owned it and he let us use it whenever we needed somewhere quiet. It was surrounded by a high wall, and a strong gate.

He went there to pray, but we couldn't keep our

eyes open. We were exhausted. We were really down and just couldn't go on. We only heard snippets of what he prayed. He was in an awful state – praying that he wouldn't have to drink 'this cup' as he called it. But he said to his Father, 'Your will be done.'

The next thing we knew he was waking us. He was completely calm again, but he said the traitor was at the gate. And we could hear voices outside and see the glow of torches. We jumped up then all right, but we were still in a kind of daze – it was as if it was a nightmare.

Jesus went straight to the gate and opened it. That was the bravest thing I've ever seen, because he knew exactly what was going to happen.

Judas was there. He came up as bold as brass to kiss Jesus, to show which one to arrest, but Jesus looked him straight in the eye and said, 'Judas, are you betraying me with a kiss?' I've never seen anyone look so miserable as Judas looked at that moment.

Then Jesus asked them, 'Who are you looking for?' And they shouted, 'Jesus of Nazareth! Which one of you is Jesus?' (Because we were all cowering behind him.) 'I am!' said Jesus, and they all fell back like snarling dogs that had been struck on the muzzle. Never had my friend looked more like a king! At that moment, if he'd wanted, he could have walked right through the crowd of them and they'd have parted like water before the prow of a ship, as I had seen him do once before at the top of a cliff in Nazareth. But that's not what he wanted. He'd said, 'No one takes my life from me. I have power to lay it down and power to take it again.'

He said, 'If you're looking for me, let these men go.' Laying down his life for his friends! Friends who didn't deserve it – who didn't even deserve to be his friends!

But Simon would have none of it. He pushed past Jesus in the gateway, swept out his sword and nearly took a man's head off. In the event it was just his ear, and Jesus healed it on the spot. Strange thing that. They all saw it – what Jesus did – but they still arrested him and dragged him away.

I'm ashamed to say we all made a run for it then – even Simon, who'd said that he would die for him. But Jesus had told him that before the cock crew in the morning he would deny that he even knew him, three times. I think that's what made Simon turn back. Jesus' words were burning in him like a fire. He couldn't leave him. He felt so ashamed. We all did. And I went back with him. But we followed at a safe distance – right into the courtyard of the High Priest's house. I had some connections there. It would have been better for Simon if we hadn't gone. Right away people thought they recognised him, and he started denying that he knew Jesus. Now don't get me wrong. Simon always was a brave man – one of the bravest. But there was something devilish about that night. We were terrified.

And all the time we were hearing what was happening to Jesus. The religious leaders put him on trial. It was completely illegal, of course, to conduct a trial in the middle of the night. They had set up the witnesses too, but even then they couldn't get their stories right. They were forced to get him to condemn himself. The High Priest asked him if he was the Son of God. And Jesus said, 'I am'. They condemned him to death for blasphemy, but what else could he say? He always told the truth.

When they led him out to take him to the Council Hall to be sentenced, it was the darkest hour, right before the dawn. It was obvious they'd been battering him. That's when Peter disowned him for the third time. And right then the cock crew, and Jesus looked straight at Simon. It was a look that would have broken your heart. And it broke Simon's heart. He went out sobbing. It's a terrible thing to see a grown man cry. Nothing I could say could comfort him. From then I was on my own.

I followed the guards and officials who led Jesus away. They took him first to the Council Hall and then to the Governor's palace to be sentenced to death. And because they wouldn't enter the house of a heathen, the Governor had to come out to them. So I could hear what was going on. Gradually quite a crowd gathered as word got round. But I didn't like the look of them. They seemed very different from the crowds that had welcomed Jesus to the city only a week before – shouting his praises to the rooftops, when he came riding on a donkey. There were some plausible people going round saying the authorities had eventually found out the truth about Jesus. Rumours were spreading round the crowd like wildfire.

The governor, Pontius Pilate, was not best pleased. He despised our religious leaders at the best of times, and the fact he had to come out to them only made it worse. He would have let Jesus go just to spite them. But they were clever. There was no talk now of blasphemy. It was all political now. They were charging him with claiming to be a king. So Pilate had to deal with it. He took Jesus inside. We heard later what happened. Pilate could see through it all. He knew Jesus was innocent. He said so when he came back out. But he said something to Jesus inside that had we known it then, we'd have known it was all over. Jesus was saying that he had come into the world to tell the truth. Pilate was going out the door and he said, 'What is truth?' – cynically, like he already knew the answer, that there's no such thing as 'The Truth'. It's bad enough when your judges don't know the difference between truth and falsehood, but when they don't believe there is such a thing as truth, you can give up hope of justice.

He tried everything, Pilate. He tried the 'release a prisoner on a holiday' card. He gave the crowd the choice of Jesus or Barabbas, who really was a political revolutionary. To his dismay, the crowd yelled for Barabbas – the rumour-mongers had done their work.

Then he tried the 'give them a taste of blood' card.

He got the soldiers to flog Jesus. It grieves me to the heart to think of it. The body that contained that great loving heart, beaten to a bloody pulp. And they mocked him. They even put a mock crown on him – a crown of thorns. Pilate brought him out to the crowd like that. If he thought they would be satisfied with that, he was wrong. Because at that moment Jesus, mocked and beaten and bloodied though he as, looked more kingly than all their governors, kings and emperors. There was a quiet nobility and a heart-rending compassion about him that all could see. No wonder Pilate said, 'Behold the man!'

That seemed to drive the crowd mad. They started shouting 'Crucify him!' The priests started it and the crowd took it up. They wanted more blood. But still Pilate wouldn't give in. He was especially frightened when he heard them say Jesus claimed to be the Son of God. He wanted to let him go then. But that's when the priests played their final card. 'Anyone who claims to be a king is an enemy of the Emperor in Rome. If you let this man go, you're not the Emperor's friend.'

So finally, Pilate condemned him. After all, what is truth? He knew he had blood on his hands, because he got water and washed his hands in front of the crowd. He said, 'I'm innocent of this man's blood!' But there's no water that can wash away that blood.

The soldiers led Jesus out of the city to the Hill of the Skull. They made him carry his own cross. He was so weak, he needed help along the way. But they finally got him there and they crucified him. They drove great iron spikes through his hands and feet into the cross – those feet that had taken him all over that land doing good – those hands that had gently healed the sick, touched the leper and raised a dead girl. That's what the world thought of all that now.

They raised him on the cross then and I remembered something he'd said. 'When I am lifted up from the earth, I will draw everyone to myself.' And certainly a crowd was gathering – but for all the wrong reasons. They had come to mock. Again the priests gave the lead. They said things like, 'If you're God's Son, prove it. Come down from the cross. Let's see one of your miracles now, Jesus.' They hadn't been so brave the day he cleared the temple – the day he overturned the tables of the corrupt money-exchange the priests had going. He ran them out of there. 'It's supposed to be a House of Prayer for all the nations,' he said, 'and you've made it a den of thieves.' No one could withstand him that day. But it's strange how brave people are when someone is helpless on a cross.

'He saved others; himself he cannot save,' they said. No, that they couldn't deny – that he'd saved others. It was only later we realised that by his not saving himself, he was saving others in an even greater way. Strange, isn't it, how often truth is spoken in jest?

He was there from nine in the morning to three in the afternoon – just six hours, but it seemed like an eternity – the mockery, the soldiers gambling for his clothes, Pilate's little joke of putting a notice on the cross saying 'Jesus of Nazareth, King of the Jews'. But through all the darkness shone Jesus' love. In the midst of his agony (of spirit as well as body) he took time to speak to the women who were weeping; to pray that the soldiers nailing him to the cross would be forgiven; to promise one of the criminals being crucified with him that he would be in heaven with him that very day; even to speak to me to ask me to look after his mother (we were there near the cross at the end – we saw it all).

At twelve noon, with the sun at its zenith, it went dark, and it stayed dark until three o'clock. To this day no one knows what caused that. But it was a darkness that was more than physical because right at that moment, Jesus yelled out, 'My God, my God, why have you forsaken me?' It sent shivers down your spine. The one who knew God as his own Father was in darkness. He cried out, 'I thirst!' And it was a thirst that no water or wine could quench. The one who told others to come to him to drink freely of the water of life and they would never thirst again, now had a raging thirst that nothing could satisfy.

His last word was this: 'It's finished'. But not what you might think. Not the whisper of a crushed and broken man. Not the bitter cry of the defeated and the disappointed. No other words can describe it but a shout of triumph! The word he used means 'Done! Completed! Paid in full!' It was like the roar of a lion, like a peal of thunder, like the trumpet heralding the new day. And at that moment just as he died, the light returned. It was a new day!

Actually there was only a few hours of sunlight left, and before dusk the soldiers had to ensure those crucified were all dead. When they came to Jesus, they saw he was already dead. But just to make sure, one of them stuck his spear into Jesus' side – just where he'd held little children close to him when he'd blessed them. And a strange thing happened – out poured blood and water. Dr Lucas explained it to me much later – it was proof positive that Jesus was dead. But the only thing in my mind then (and now) is that he said his blood would be poured out so that the sins of many people would be forgiven.

Many years before, one of our prophets foretold that they would look on the one they had pierced, and that that day a fountain would be opened in Jerusalem for sin and for uncleanness. That day I saw the fountain opened.

Three years before, I was there that day when John the Baptiser had pointed to Jesus and said 'Look, the Lamb of God who takes away the sin of the world!' I now know what he meant. No more need for lamb's blood smeared on our doors. No more need for signs and symbols and shadows. The reality has come. 'The blood of Jesus Christ cleanses us from all sin.'

Not long ago Jesus gave me a vision of heaven – they were all dressed in white robes. How did they get there? I was told they had washed their robes and made them white in the blood of the Lamb.

You can wash and be clean in the blood of the Lamb. All you have to do is trust in the blood – his blood that sealed his covenant of love. Whoever believes in him will never perish but have eternal life.

We didn't realise all that then. We didn't remember all he had taught us – not until we saw him again (but that's another story). That night was a dark night, the darkest I'd ever known. Even the moon turned red, blood red. And Simon remembered the words of the prophet Joel: 'The sun will be turned to darkness and the moon to blood before the coming of the great and glorious day of the Lord. And everyone who calls on the name of the Lord will be saved.'

# 12
# No Really Satisfactory Explanation?

The real reason I was sent to Jerusalem as the stand-in Governor was to tidy up after the mess left by Pontius Pilate. Things had got so bad that Vitellius, Governor of Syria, had to order Pilate to return to Rome to report to Caesar. Luckily for him, Tiberius Caesar died before he got there – or perhaps not so luckily, as it turned out.

Vitellius sent me, his friend, Marcellus, to investigate and report to Rome. He appointed me as a special Imperial investigator. Before I went up to Jerusalem, I came straight down to Caesarea and managed to catch Pilate before he left for Rome. It was strange. He seemed different altogether from his reputation as a hard man. He was, after all, a military man like myself.

For one thing, I couldn't get much sense out of him. I tried to interview him about the various complaints that were made against him over the ten years he was governor of Judea: provoking the Jews by taking the standards of the legions into the holy city of Jerusalem; or building an aqueduct with temple money and then slaughtering a large number who protested against that during a religious festival (they came to be known as those whose blood Pilate had mingled with their sacrifices); or the final straw, attacking another religious group called Samaritans when they gathered on Mount Gerizim hoping to find the lost ark of the covenant – some object of veneration both for the Jews and Samaritans. The Jews claimed it had been in their temple in Jerusalem. But when the Roman general Pompey took Jerusalem, he entered the very heart of the temple and reported the strange fact that there was nothing there! No idol, no image of a god. Just an empty room!

Anyway, it was this Samaritan incident that finally did for Pilate, but when I questioned him about all that and tried to get at the truth, he grimaced and said, 'But what is the truth?' with an emphasis on *the truth*. And whenever I mentioned any of these killings, he would just say, 'Yes, blood! You and I have seen a lot of blood in our time.' Then he would fix me with his glassy stare and say, 'But there's blood, and blood.'

The breakthrough (if you could call it that) came when I asked him about a strange habit he had. He was always washing his hands. I thought it might have been something that he had picked up in the East. He was silent for a long time. Then he said, 'I've blood on my hands.' I thought he meant the Jews and Samaritans, but he said, 'No! Not them! They hated me, the lot of them!'

He started looking furtively from side to side and asked if he could speak to me privately. Well, I agreed, as we seemed to be getting somewhere at last. He then told me something I have never forgotten. In fact it has nagged at me all these years. At the time I didn't know what to think. I wondered if Pilate had gone mad. There's no doubt that he was mentally disturbed, but you know when someone is being completely honest.

He told me about this prisoner he had to deal with – about six years before. The Jewish authorities had hauled him up before him on a capital charge – treason. They said he was claiming to be King of the Jews. Now Pilate was quite convinced the man was just some sort of religious teacher that had fallen out with the authorities over some obscure point of their traditions, and was not guilty of any capital offence. But no matter how he tried, he couldn't satisfy them.

This man came from Galilee where Herod Antipas was ruler. So he sent him to Herod, but *he* couldn't find fault with him. Pilate asked the crowd if they wanted him set free, but they chose another man, a real criminal by the name of Barabbas. He had this preacher flogged, but that didn't satisfy them. They even said he claimed to be the Son of God! (You could see that even all these years later that still shook Pilate. I understood that fully only later.) He tried everything he could to get them to see sense, but in the end they threatened to inform Caesar that he was going to release a dangerous political rebel. 'So what could I do?' Pilate said to me, 'I was in enough trouble already.' Finally he washed his hands of it (literally) saying he was innocent of this man's blood, but he handed him over to be crucified. Strange for such a hard man, but you could see that this still haunted him.

But the strangest thing happened when I was leaving. Pilate's wife, Claudia Procula, collared me on the way out and said that she was sure her husband hadn't told me the most important thing. I was in a hurry and I thought she was trying to tell me about a dream she'd had about this preacher (Pilate had told me all about it), but she took me aside and said no, it was something else. She asked me if I knew about the empty tomb. This was news to me! I hadn't much time – I was due to leave for Jerusalem the next day – but as far as I could make her out, this was the story. After this preacher – Iesous, she called him – was crucified, he was actually buried in a rich man's tomb, but on the third day, the tomb was empty, and although various stories were going around, there was no really satisfactory explanation.

I must say, at the time, I discounted all this as the product of a woman's feverish imagination. But when I arrived in Jerusalem (after a rather tedious journey, I must say) I found this was still a matter of some controversy. It appeared that the movement of this Iesous, instead of dying out after his death, had actually gone from strength to strength. His followers were convinced he had actually returned from the grave. Some of them claimed to have met him. And when this message was proclaimed, thousands of people believed it! By the time I arrived, it appeared that things had quietened down. A persecution had arisen against them, because one of their young hotheads called Stephen had offended the authorities (just like his master) by insisting that there was no longer any need for their Temple, because this Iesous was the only way to God – they just had one God. The crowd then stoned this Stephen to death, with the full approval of the authorities, which was all most irregular. It was obvious that by this time Pilate had lost the plot altogether. I afterwards discovered that what had really happened was not that these Iesous people had died out, but that a lot of them had been scattered all over the world. But I'll come back to that later.

I'll admit that I had originally been intrigued about the whole thing because of Pilate and the strange transformation that had come over him, but once I was at the scene of the crime, so to speak, and everywhere I went it kept cropping up, the more intrigued I became. I could justify the amount of time I started spending on this aspect of Pilate's case, because it was obvious something had happened to unbalance him, but deep down I wanted to find the truth for myself.

The first real opportunity I got was when I was talking to some of the religious leaders – those who had held the office of High Priest – about their complaints against Pilate. Once I had dealt with that, I asked them about this other matter. At first they were cagey, but when I indicated that I considered it highly relevant to the case, they opened up and told me in no uncertain terms that this Iesous had claimed a political title – Christos, the Anointed King – which was a title from one of their ancient prophetical writings. So I said to them, 'And he was not this Christos?' It was only a fraction of a second, but they hesitated, before vehemently denying it.

After confirming that in their opinion Pilate had definitely been strangely reluctant to order the execution, I asked about another irregularity – the burial. Only when I stressed that it was highly irregular that an executed criminal who was not a Roman citizen should be granted a burial, did they admit that two of their leading citizens had got permission from Pilate to bury him. I made a note of their names – Joseph from Arimathea and Nicodemus – and where to find them.

Then I quizzed them on the stories that were circulating about the empty tomb. At this they affected an air of boredom, and said that people knew right from the start the truth of the matter, but the common people prefer legends to the plain truth. The truth was, they said, that some of the followers of this Iesous came secretly at night and removed the body. 'And you were not able to apprehend these grave-robbers?' I asked. They assured me that although strenuous efforts were made, from that day to this, no culprits and no body were ever found. But seven weeks later, some of his followers emerged from hiding and started proclaiming in the Temple precincts that this Iesous had actually come back from the grave and they had seen him.

A few days later, when I visited Nicodemus, he was rather alarmed to see a high ranking Roman official with a detachment of soldiers. When I assured him that they were for my safety, not for his arrest, he relaxed and welcomed me most hospitably, which surprised me, as these Jews had strange laws about welcoming foreigners. After a time I broached the reason for my visit, and he immediately became nervous again, but I told him he had nothing to fear if he told me the truth. He then confirmed that he had helped his friend Joseph to bury Iesous (although he called him the Lord Iesous). He stressed that this was only after Joseph had got permission from Pilate and they had buried him in Joseph's own tomb, which had been recently hewn out of the rock. This piece of information was news to me and I asked if he could show me the tomb. Nicodemus then sent a message to Joseph and we met at the actual tomb.

Joseph described to me how he had gone to Pilate to ask for the body of Iesous. He said it was the least he could do. (I took it that both he and Nicodemus had become followers of Iesous.) And he added this interesting piece of information: Pilate was surprised to hear that Iesous was already dead. This reminded me of one of my own suspicions – that Iesous had not really been dead when he was put in the tomb, and later emerged alive. I thought it highly unlikely, knowing the efficiency of our soldiers in execution, but one had to cover all possibilities. Joseph assured me that Pilate had called the centurion responsible who confirmed that Iesous had died, and both Joseph and Nicodemus confirmed that they had spent a long time preparing the body for burial with grave-clothes and perfumed spices, and there was no doubt that Iesous was dead, but I made a mental note to find the centurion.

Then the tomb itself was very interesting. It was closed by a large flat disc of stone over six feet in diameter, which had obviously been rolled down a narrow channel in the rock until it dropped into place. I asked if the grave had been reused since. Joseph assured me that it was as empty as the day Iesous had risen from the dead. My curiosity was then greatly aroused, and I asked if it would be possible to open the tomb. They looked at each other and said it would take ten strong men to open it, but Joseph would arrange it if I insisted. I did, and he did, the next day. Nicodemus even offered to contact some of the witnesses to the risen Iesous to ask them to meet me, an offer I gladly accepted.

Meanwhile, I went in search of the centurion. Amazingly, I found him! He had actually returned to

Jerusalem after service elsewhere. He remembered the case quite clearly. In fact he said he would never forget it. He would never forget the animosity of the religious leaders against Iesous (only he also called him the Lord Iesous). He would never forget the mysterious darkness that fell at noon as he was being crucified. But most of all, he would never forget the way the crucified man conducted himself – prayed for his executioners, gave comfort to a fellow condemned man and endured depths of despair before dying in apparent victory!

'Was he really dead?' He repeated my question. 'That was the strangest thing of a strange day. People don't die of crucifixion in six hours! I've seen strong men last for days (and he was a strong man). We had to take our hammers to the other two to finish them off, but he was already dead. He died with a loud shout, "It is paid in full!" I didn't know what he meant then.'

'But surely,' I said, 'If you didn't break his legs, he could have been still alive!' He looked grim. 'No one lives after having a Roman spear stuck in their heart. That's what one of my men did just to make sure. It was obvious he was dead already, because his heart wasn't pumping out fresh blood. There was just this clotted blood and watery stuff. No, he was dead all right.'

I then asked him what he thought about the empty tomb and the story that his followers had removed the body. He said, 'You mean, you don't know? That was a story invented by the religious authorities. I knew the soldiers that guarded the tomb.'

This was definitely news to me! 'What guard?' He told me all about how the authorities had asked Pilate to provide a guard for the tomb, because Iesous had said that he would rise from the dead. In the early morning while it was still dark, there was this tremendous roar and a blinding light and the guards were paralysed with fright. When they came to themselves, the huge stone was rolled back and the tomb was empty apart from the grave-clothes. They fled back into the city and there the religious leaders invented a story for them. They told them to say the followers of Iesous had come while they were asleep and stolen the body. They also paid them a tidy sum for their co-operation and promised to keep them out of trouble with Pilate.

Before I left the centurion, I asked him what he thought about it all himself. He looked me in the eye and said, 'I say now what I said that day at the foot of his cross, 'This man was the Son of God!'

I had a lot to think about that night. My questions were moving from Pilate and his role in the affair, and even from the mysterious empty tomb, more to this character Iesous, who seemed to have such a powerful effect on everyone.

The next day I met Joseph and Nicodemus again. Not only did they have a large group of workmen with them, but also one striking looking man. He was a big strong man.

While the workmen set to work with various

implements, I was introduced to the other follower of Iesous – Petros, the big man, who had been a fisherman.

Petros explained how he had followed Iesous for three years before he had died. He had heard him give wonderful teaching, and he had seen him perform various miracles and show great love to all the people. But when the authorities had arrested Iesous, all of his followers had forsaken him. Petros himself had even disowned him. When their teacher had been crucified, they thought it was the end. The end of all their dreams. They were not expecting a happy ending.

'But did you,' I asked him directly, 'did you come with accomplices, roll away this stone and steal the body?'

'Sir,' he said, 'We couldn't have rolled away a pebble, such was our distress and disappointment!'

'So you can imagine our astonishment,' he continued, 'when on the third day, some of our women who had been early to the tomb to see if they could anoint the body, came running back to tell us the stone had been rolled away! Well, me and my friend John, we fairly ran here, and although my friend arrived first (he's younger and fitter than me), a fear and a wonder came over him and he did not enter. I was the first to go in. But we both saw it. It wasn't just that the tomb was empty. It was the grave-clothes. They weren't all messed about as if people had hastily removed the body. They were lying, well,

133

as if they had collapsed themselves when there was no body inside them!'

I saw what he was implying, but I was impressed with his account. He didn't try to pretend he had seen the actual rising of the dead man.

By this time the workmen had finally managed to get the stone back up the groove in the rock leaving the entrance to the tomb open. Petros showed exactly where he had stood and where the grave-clothes were. It gave me an eerie feeling standing there, as Petros went on to tell of how he had seen Iesous again. They had been meeting in secret for fear of the authorities with the doors and windows locked, when Iesous had stood among them. It was the same Iesous. He even showed them the marks of the nails in his hands and feet. He even ate some food with them. He was no ghost. But he was different. No mere mortal could appear and disappear at will. And it was not his imagination. Over five hundred people had seen the Lord Iesous at one time. Petros said he was risen from the dead with power. And they experienced that power seven weeks later when he sent the Spirit of Power and Petros preached to a huge crowd in Jerusalem and three thousand people became followers of Iesous. And now even one of their greatest enemies, who had tried to destroy them, had met the risen Lord and become a follower. I had heard rumours of this Saul of Tarsus before and would have liked to meet him.

However, I had one last question for Joseph and

Nicodemus, as I felt a natural reluctance to accept what was being said. 'Perhaps the explanation is that your authorities, or even Pilate, removed the body for safe keeping?'

Nicodemus smiled and said, 'It is theoretically possible. But if they did, all they needed to do to stop so many following the Lord was to produce the body! That they have never done!'

By the time I returned to Rome with my report I found the new Emperor Caligula had lost interest, because in my absence Pilate had committed suicide and as far as the Emperor was concerned, that was the end of it. It was his successor, Claudius, who actually showed some interest. Although he was physically disabled, his mind was as sharp as a razor, and he had a great interest in all things religious and particularly in the Jews.

However, he didn't really understand my report. I suppose he couldn't accept what I have since come to accept. What he did decide to do was issue an edict. You can read it still. It was inscribed on a stone tablet and stands in Nazareth, the home town of the Lord Iesous. This is what it says:

*ORDINANCE OF CAESAR*

*It is my pleasure that graves and tombs remain undisturbed in perpetuity for those who have made them for the cult of their ancestors, or children, or members of their house. If, however, any man lay information that another has either demolished them, or has in any other way extracted the buried, or has maliciously transferred them to other places in order to wrong them, or has displaced the sealing or other stones, against such a one I order that a trial be instituted, as in respect of the gods, so in regard to the cult of mortals. For it shall be much more obligatory to honour the buried. Let it be absolutely forbidden for anyone to disturb them. In the case of contravention I desire that the offender be sentenced to capital punishment on charge of violation of sepulture.*

I think he missed the point.

## Tell me the old, old story

Tell me the old, old story
    Of unseen things above,
Of Jesus and His glory,
    Of Jesus and His love.

Tell me the story simply
    As to a little child;
For I am weak and weary,
    And helpless and defiled.

Tell me the story slowly,
    That I may take it in –
That wonderful redemption,
    God's remedy for sin.

Tell me the story often,
    For I forget so soon;
The early dew of morning
    Has passed away at noon.

Tell me the story softly,
    With earnest tones and grave;
Remember I'm the sinner
    Christ Jesus came to save.

Tell me the story always
    If you would really be,
In any time of trouble,
    A comforter to me.

*Tell me the same old story*
  *When you have cause to fear*
*That this world's empty glory*
  *Is costing me too dear.*

*Yes, and when that world's glory*
  *Shall dawn upon my soul,*
*Tell me the old, old story,*
  *'Christ Jesus makes you whole.'*

*Kate Hankey (1834-1911)*

# Postscript

I have always been fascinated by the stories of the Bible. A large part of the Bible is in fact narrative. No doubt the stories of the Bible have influenced the development of narrative in Western literature. But stories are loved in all cultures and by all ages and classes of people – witness the popularity of stories in film, television and novels. The love of story is part of our humanness. We are, after all, created in the image of God, who is the Author of the greatest story ever told.

It is that greatest story that fascinates me the most. In this book I have tried to retell aspects of that story as seen through the eyes of some of the eyewitnesses. Mostly these are real eyewitnesses mentioned in the Bible, or by the Jewish historian Josephus; in two cases the story-teller is purely imaginary (interestingly one of these was the first story I attempted).

The stories originated not as part of a book, but as stories told to an audience. I am a preacher, and I am always thinking of ways of engaging my audience. It occurred to me that as preachers we mostly think of engaging people's reason, emotions and will, and all three are important aspects of our humanity. But the element that so often is neglected is the imagination. The preachers that engage people's imagination, however, are usually effective communicators. We can see this every time a preacher tells a story to illustrate a point. Attentions that before were wandering are immediately recaptured!

This once struck me forcibly in a different way in listening to a colleague preach. He was preaching through a narrative passage, but by engaging the imagination he made you feel you were there! I had preached in something like that style myself, probably more often in my younger days in the ministry, and it made me want to explore it again.

The occasion was a guest service. These are services (usually Sunday evening) which our church runs on roughly a monthly basis throughout the year. The idea is that people are encouraged to invite friends along to hear the preacher speak of some of the central truths of the Christian faith and what it means to become a Christian.

I wanted to preach about 'the sinful woman' (Luke 7) who washed Jesus' feet with her tears, and I wanted to engage people's imagination in the story. At some point in preparation, the thought suddenly came to me, 'Why not just tell the story?' This I attempted to do, using an imaginary visitor to the house telling the story in the present tense as it unfolded before his eyes (a technique I have not used again). The impact of telling the story to an audience was such that I felt I was on to something important, and I have since tried to develop the technique.

It has been interesting that many different people have appreciated this style of expounding and applying God's word, but perhaps particularly significant has been the fact that it appears that these stories have been particularly appreciated by women, children and young people – in fact those whom male preachers often find difficulty in engaging.

To those who may wonder about my Biblical warrant for substituting these stories for sermons, all I would say is that Jesus told stories, and God in his wisdom couched a large part of his revelation in narrative form.

Two further things need to be said. First, in some cases I have let my imagination go too far perhaps for some people's liking. My only justification is that I feel I have not done much more than what a good preacher would do in answering such a question as: 'What might have been the reasons for this person acting in the way he or she did?'

For instance, in the case of Joanna, all Luke says about her problem is she was one of the women who 'had been cured of evil spirits and diseases'. I tried to imagine what kind of illness or evil she might have had, and came up with alcoholism. Of course it is completely possible that it was not that at all. But in a sermon, the preacher might say, 'Imagine Joanna's problem was alcoholism and how she would have felt when Jesus freed her from it.' These stories are not exact copies of the biblical stories (which would make them just paraphrases) – they are more like sermons in a different form.

Second, one of the main purposes in telling these stories is to encourage people to read the original stories in the Bible. While some aspects of my retelling of these stories may be purely imaginary, the original stories are sober historical fact. I believe not only that they are the carefully recorded accounts of eyewitnesses, but also that the authors were kept from error by the Holy Spirit of God. It is these accounts, part of the greatest story ever told, which give the message of hope and love and eternal life.

Alex J. MacDonald

# The Biblical Stories

Chapters in this book with corresponding Biblical passages

1. Luke 1 and 2
2. Matthew 2
3. Luke 3, John 1, Luke 7:18-35, Mark 6:14-29, Luke 8:1-3, John 10:40-42, Luke 24:1-12
4. John 4:1-42
5. Luke 7:36-50
6. Matthew 8:23-34, Mark 4:35–5:20, Luke 8:22-39
7. Matthew 9:18-26, Mark 5:21-43, Luke 8:40-56
8. Matthew 16:13-17:13, Mark 8:27–9:13, Luke 9:18-36
9. Matthew 19:16-30, Mark 10:17-31, Luke18:18-30
10. Mark 10:46-52, Luke 15:1-32, 18:35–19:10
11. All four Gospel accounts of the last hours of Jesus' life, together with 1 John.
12. All four Gospel accounts of the death and resurrection of Jesus.